The Politics of *Windrush*

KENT·INSTITUTE
OF·ART·&·DESIGN
LIBRARY

The Politics of *Windrush*

PETER FRYER

Index Books
*in association with the Black Cultural Archives,
the Movement for Socialism,
and Leeds Independent Labour Network*

Published by Index Books (Indexreach Ltd.)
10-12 Atlantic Road SW9 8HY. Tel: 0171-274 8342

Typeset by Sumner Type, London SE22
Printed by Trade Union Printing Services, Newcastle upon Tyne

Pictures: Personal photos, Black Cultural Archives, Churches
Commission for Racial Justice, London Transport Museum, West
Indian Ex-Servicemen and Women's Association, Sia, and others

Cover design: Brian Eley

304.8 FRY

A C.I.P. catalogue record for this book is available from the British
Library

ISBN: 1-871518-24-5

Awaiting departure on the Empire Windrush

This is an edited version of a talk given at the Mandela Centre, Leeds, on 10 September 1998 under the auspices of the Leeds Independent Labour Network, and at Lambeth Town Hall, Brixton, on 20 November 1998 under the auspices of the Black Cultural Archives, Index Bookcentre, and the Movement for Socialism.

1

Sketch map of the West Indies

EMPIRE ¦WINDRUSH ●

LONDON ⟂

The Politics of *Windrush*

Lambeth Town Hall, Friday 20 November 1998

'Brixton makes history, not only for Britain, but also internationally,' said *Sam Walker of the Black Cultural Archives*, opening the meeting. 'A lot of people come over in the summer time and because of what they have heard, they want to know more about Brixton and its people. Looking around we can see quite a lot of us, all of us from different backgrounds, from the same race — the human race — but we've got different skin colours: black, white, brown, etc. Quite a mixture. Lambeth is a uniting borough.

'I want to acknowledge the presence of the elders: Mr Christopher Columbus [Oswald Denniston] came on the *Windrush* and had a stall in Brixton market. He is one of the oldest stallholders in the market. Mr Allan Wilmot came here before the *Windrush* — he is a second-world-war veteran. Mr Leroy Gittens is the public relations officer for the West Indian Ex-Servicemen's Association. Mother Nadia Cattouse was an actress who became a teacher and has been a leading member engaging in the struggle for black people over many years.

'I can see some older white people who must have shared in the struggle against racism and stereotyping of black people. I believe their presence here tells us quite a lot, that as black and white people we can work together in solving our problems.

'There are also quite a lot of young people. I'm delighted to see them all here. When you leave this meeting you'll have a lot of information which you can use for your course work or take back to your parents. More important, you'll take back with you a lot of information so that as you grow into adulthood you'll be able to pass whatever history you learn here today to your children.

'It is good to see you all.'

Leroy Gittens of the West Indian Ex-Servicemen and Women's Association

Our association goes back about 27 years. We filled a void that Social Security has left. Because we're ex-servicemen I feel we're smarter than the average civilian, so we jumped in there quick to look after the elderly people. Our association is not open to black people alone, it's open to all races and all ages. Any young persons who want to visit us, just give me a call. I will lay on a show, pictures, videos ... and we welcome groups from schools.

At the meeting in Brixton: Chair Sam Walker, Leroy Gittens of the West Indian Ex-Servicemen and Women's Association, and Peter Fryer

I am not of the *Windrush* generation. I am an ex-serviceman. I did six years from 1962 to 1968. I served in the Far East, in Borneo, as an insructor. I've brought one flash-card with me today because I came from a school. It simply says: 'The War Effort in the West Indies' and it tells you that at the outbreak of war all the crops and industries in the West Indies were modified to prosecute the war in Britain. So they contribute manpower, skills, expenses, oil, rum, sugar, cocoa, bananas and limes, and medical supplies.

I'll take you back to bananas. A few years ago if you talked about bananas there was this negative attitude to bananas. Take a trip to space and bananas is the only solid food you can take. Even NASA scientists discover something good about bananas.

Over £75,000 to the UK for general war purposes. Over 1 million troops from the West Indies alone. Nearly £400,000 for war charities, essential munitions and raw materials such as oil and bauxite. £425,000 for the purchase of aircraft.

Yes, we did have black fighter pilots and black bomber crews,

The War Effort In The West Indies

Considering their size, the West Indian islands played a tremendous role in World War II. For such a small and relatively poor part of the British Empire, the people and Governments of the region provided substantial assistance, completely orientating their economies to the needs of Britain and the USA. They contributed manpower, skills, money towards defraying war expenses and vital munitions such as oil for the Navy, rum for the men in the North Sea and the trenches, tropical plantation crops such as sugar, cocoa, bananas and limes and medical supplies. A breakdown of some of these contributions is as follows:

* Over £75 000 to the UK for general war purposes

* Over 1 million troops

* Nearly £400 000 for war charities

* Essential munitions and raw materials such as oil and bauxite

* £425 000 for the purchase of aircrafts for the RAF

* Investment in war Bonds

* An interest free loan of £1.400 000

* Surgical supplies

* Food and clothing for British Forces

Throughout the war, German submarines ravaged the Atlantic shipping lanes (the West Indian Islands are surrounded by the Caribbean Sea and the Atlantic Ocean), prowled ports and torpedoed ships.

The region was a particularly important target for German submarines seeking to disrupt traffic travelling through the Panama Canal between the Atlantic and Pacific Oceans. Also under constant menace were the Caribbean's oil installations. Because of this submarine presence, by 1941 the Caribbean was considered one of the most dangerous places in the world for the passage shipping.

Poster from the West Indian Ex-Servicemen and Women's Association

although if you watch the Battle of Britain you'll never see that.

But *Windrush* [anniversary] has been a great thing. It sort of brings it into the open and since *Windrush* I've been busy going from school to school all up and down the length and breadth of England telling them about our association.

Investment in war bonds: an interest-free loan of £1,400,000. Go back to the 1940s and convert it to today's currency and add the interest on. We're talking about serious repayment of the national debts. This was interest-free! So, yes, I think Britain does owe a lot to the West Indies and Caribbean.

You all heard about lend-lease where America loaned Britain some rusty battleships and in return Britain gave them prize islands in the West Indies to act as bases. These are things people from the West Indies contributed. Surgical supplies, food and clothing for British forces.

Somewhere along the line to my white compatriots there, my parents probably fed your parents. So we've got a lot in common considering we served under the same flag. We all spoke English even though it's difficult to listen to someone from Liverpool or Scotland or even Yorkshire. You don't know what you go through, and it's still English! But again, we don't hold it against them, we don't criticise them because of their dialect. We just acknowledge that they're slightly different and we understand, because we're tolerant people.

We're so tolerant that when people talk about being black I laugh. I'll tell you why. Being an ex-serviceman I find it funny because any time you go into combat, you know what's the first thing you do? You get yourself black. You blacken up your face because black is a colour of survival and they survive because they become black. We survived because we were born black and we know what it is to survive.

Thanks for listening. I'm available for anyone that wants to speak to me.

WEST INDIAN EX-SERVICEMEN AND WOMEN'S
ASSOCIATION (UK)
161-167 CLAPHAM MANOR STREET, LONDON, SW4 6DB
Telephone: 0171-627-0702

*"Never in the
field of human
conflict was,
so much owed,
by so many,
to so few"*

Sir Winston
Churchill

THE CARIBBEAN EFFORT
IN WORLD WAR II

Members of West Indian A.T.S. at an Army Camp serving in World War II.

Both men and women from the Caribbean fought in the British army.

THE DECISION TO RESCIND THE COLOUR BAR

When Cabinet first began discussing colonial manpower in 1939, the Secretary for the Colonies reported that though there was a "wave of intense loyalty in the West Indies, this may not be maintained unless suitable openings can be found for utilising the numerous offers of service for military and other duties."

The Colonial Office had a vested interest in bringing pressure to bear on the armed services to lift the colour bar. It was responsible for controlling the Empire and ensuring that while Britain was fighting a war against racist Germany, She should not be accused of racist practices. Also, the recent uprisings in the Caribbean left it uneasy, the Colonial Office could not afford to risk further revolt as a result of the colour bar. It would have been politically and practically disastrous to send troops to control rebellious British subjects while Britain was herself engaged in supposedly anti-racist war in Europe.

As the war progressed, the shortage of skilled labour was another factor which served to work against the continuance of the colour bar. It was estimated that between June and December 1941 the armed forces would need 25,835 skilled engineers, but that only 8,660 men would be available. The Ministry of Labour therefore decided to import workers from the West Indies for training for the munitions industry.

By August 1942, the shortage had become so great that the Army decided to accept "coloured tradesmen". The RAF followed suit, but the Navy still preferred "not to consider any coloured British subjects."

The West Indian Ex-Servicemen and Women's Association has produced material about the massive Caribbean war contribution. Men and women joined the armed forces; civilians contributed in many different ways.

Mr Oswald Denniston, also known as Christopher Columbus, who arrived on Windrush *and has been the longest stallholder in Brixton market, answered questions from the audience.*

Question: What was it like on the ship itself?

Mr Denniston: If I want to speak the truth I can hardly tell you much about the ship because from the day I left Jamaica I been playing cards until I reach England. Won a few bob. It's the truth. You must can find something harder than that!

Question: Can you recall the public reaction when you appeared in Brixton as one of the stallholders?

Mr D.: It's quite strange. They accepted me. 'Shall I or shall I not?' for about the first five or ten years.

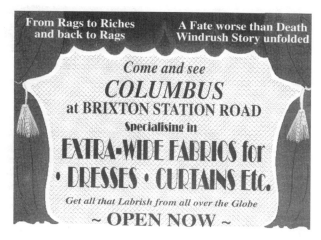

Leaflet advertising Mr Denniston's market stall

Afterwards it was perfectly OK. My trouble was the next person's trouble and their trouble was my trouble. You know how it is. If you know English people you have to expect .... Like four people working on a ceiling. Four men, three and myself, and they're talking among themselves all the time, not me included because I'm the odd man out. And one man left and went to the toilet and they've been talking all the time between themselves and they say: 'Cor! Can't stick him, can you?' [LAUGHTER]. So when you get to know that part about English people you can enjoy them. No harm. [LAUGHTER]

Please let [the questions] come. Make it worth my while because remember this is voluntary; I'm not being paid. [LAUGHTER] Take what you get for nothing!

Question: Where were you born and what part of Jamaica did you grow up in?

Mr D.: I was brought up in the same place as I was born, Montego Bay, and I left there when I was a man. Actually I was 35 years old when I left Jamaica, so I knew exactly what I was doing. The only thing I didn't do was make myself rich. [LAUGHTER]. I've got a sign I left in a little place where I was keeping some stuff and the lady says: 'Before we fall out, take this thing.' It's a sign that says: 'From rags to riches and back to rags — a fate worse than death.' Everyone thinks it's harsh but it's true. I didn't look after my money, unfortunately. I won't get any this way, so I have to start thinking from tonight what I'm going to do again because there ain't no market again.

Mr Oswald Denniston answering questions

Question: What year did you set up your stall in Brixton?
Mr D.: 1951

Question: What were the first things that surprised or shocked you when you arrived?
Mr D.: I happened to do a little signwriting and I got a job with a firm called Knight Construction in Clapham South. The boss sent me to do a fascia: 'Rose: fruiterer, florist, greengrocer', and I sat down on the trestle, working there, painting this sign, and the man who the job was belonging to tapped me on my ankle and said: 'Darkie, aren't you embarrassed?' So I said: 'What for?' I looked down at him. He said: 'All those people there watching you.' So I saw, oh, five times this amount of people on the other side of the road, almost blocking the road, watching me. So I turned to him, the gentleman who asked me if I'm not embarrassed, and I said to him: 'Why is that, then?' He blushed. He said: 'They never see your people doing this kind of work.' So I was surprised, because where I come from, whether you're blue, pink, yellow or black, if you're a signwriter, you're a

signwriter. [LAUGHTER]. So that really surprised me.
Until now I'm still really surprised to see that the average
working-class English person knows very, very little about the
colonials. Things that we learn at school, it's ridiculous when you
come to think about it, for your means of livelihood. Imagine
teaching me at school:

> *The rich man's son inherits lands and piles of bricks and stone
> and gold.*
> *He also inherits soft white hands, tender flesh that fear the
> cold, nor dare to wear a garment old.*
> *A heritage, it seem to me, one would wish to hold in fee.*
>
> *What does a poor man's son inherit?*
> *Stout muscles, sinewy heart, a king of two hands.*
> *A heritage, it seem to me, one scarce would wish to hold in fee.*

Now look at the Aga Khan's hands. Could you call the Aga Khan's
hands dark or black? His hand is soft, not hard, but they say that
because you've this skin here your hand must be white and soft! Well
I was so surprised...

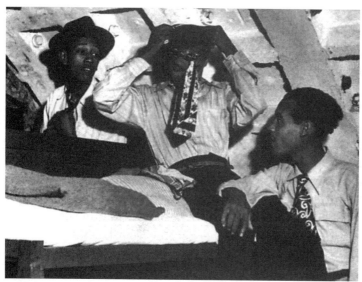

Special
coaches took
236 of the
Windrush
settlers to
Clapham
Common,
south
London,
where the
air-raid
shelter was
reopened for
their use

Many people who came on the Windrush *later settled in Brixton*

Chair: You will agree with me that the book *Staying Power* has become the 'bible' of black British history. Had it not been for that book a lot of us would have been lost about what black British history is, about how long black people have been here. When you read *Staying Power* and look at the bibliography, the references, it doesn't become anecdotal, the evidence is there. As black historians and as historians generally, people who are seeking after the truth, we are indebted to Peter Fryer's research.

Today he'll be talking about the Politics of *Windrush*. When *Windrush* arrived, Peter Fryer recorded that event for the press.

FIVE HUNDRED PAIRS OF WILLING HANDS

The Jamaicans Land in Britain

From PETER FRYER

FIVE HUNDRED pairs of willing hands grasped the rails of the Empire Windrush as she came alongside the landing stage at Tilbury early yesterday morning.

On board were 500 Jamaicans, every one of whom was eager to work in Britain.

Before they could land they had to see Colonial Office and Ministry of Labour Officials, whose job was to sort them out according to experience and ability.

By a lucky chance a Colonial Office welfare man was on the ship during the voyage and he had been able to make a rough classification.

When I went on board I asked scores of men why they had come to Britain. Practically every one gave the same answer—unemployment and low wages "back home," and the prospect of a good job in Britain.

Many of them told me that they had already spent several years here in the Forces.

I was given two interesting sidelights on the voyage itself. First came from Miss Evelyn Wauchbe, a coloured girl, who was one of eight stowaways.

When it became too cold to sleep out at night, Miss Wauchbe had to give herself up. The news spread like wildfire. Someone took the hat round, and £48 was collected to pay for a first-class fare.

Helpful

A less-pleasant story was told to me by Mrs. C. E. Monroe, of Coventry, who has returned home with her Jamaican husband after 14 months in the West Indies.

"I have come up against a good deal of prejudice from the other white passengers, among whom are 60 Polish women," she told me. "Many people have cut me because they know my husband is coloured. He himself has been openly insulted."

By contrast, the attitude of Government officials was very helpful.

The 204 West Indians who have friends in Britain have been given travel warrants to wherever they want to go, the

52 Forces volunteers will be accommodated in a Colonial Office hostel, and the remaining 236 were taken by special coaches to the Clapham South shelter.

Some 30 have volunteered for the mines, and will, I understand, be given full facilities for training.

While on board the ship I met masons, mechanics, journalists, students, musicians, boxers and cyclists attending the Olympic Games.

To-night some of the immigrants will speak at a meeting of the London branch of the Caribbean Labour Congress, to be held at the Holborn Hall, at 7 p.m.

Daily Worker, *23 June 1948*

But These Ten Only Got Ten Days

Ten Jamaicans were at Grays, Essex, yesterday each fined £1, or seven days, for travelling on the Empire Windrush without having paid their fares and sentenced to ten days' imprisonment for being stowaways, sentences to run concurrently.

WAS IT REALLY NECESSARY?

Forced to emigrate from their homeland, these puzzled-looking Jamaicans seeking work in Britain may well be asking themselves: "Was my journey really necessary," as they wait to land at Tilbury yesterday.

The Politics of *Windrush*

PETER FRYER

The Leeds meeting: Peter Fryer with Norma Hutchinson

My first words must be to pay homage, from the bottom of my heart, to the pioneers; to the first generation of post-war settlers from the Caribbean; to the men and women of the *Empire Windrush* generation.

Empire Windrush is here, of course, a figure of speech. When we celebrate the arrival of that particular ship 50 years ago last June we are celebrating also the arrival of the *Orbita*, the *Reina del Pacifico*, the *Georgic*, and all the other ships that brought settlers from the Caribbean to this country until those shameful Commonwealth Immigrants Acts of 1962 and 1968 made racism part of British law.

I am proud to honour the courage and perseverance of those young men and women who landed at Tilbury or got off the boat trains at Paddington or Victoria or Waterloo in their best suits and best dresses, who came here hoping to build a new and better life in what they had been educated — or rather, miseducated — to regard as their 'Mother Country'.

I said 'in their best suits and best dresses'. But let us not forget that some of them were in uniform, and that some of the rest had not long been out of uniform. For during the second world war of 1939-45 about 8,000 Caribbean troops had come 5,000 miles across the Atlantic to serve in Britain under the Union Jack.

Yes . . . we have a job for you. This is the opportunity you've hoped for. You will be trained by experts in any of the categories listed below FREE OF CHARGE. And what's more, you will be earning while you're learning.

All the resources of the R.A.F. will be at your disposal. Expert Physical Training, Medical care and schools with highly qualified tutors are among the many features of this training programme that has been designed to equip you for the many opportunities that the peace is sure to bring.

ONLY A LIMITED NUMBER OF MEN ARE REQUIRED! ACT TO-DAY !!

HERE ARE THE JOBS THAT ARE OPEN:-

- CLERKS—General Assistant
- EQUIPMENT ASSISTANTS
- CARPENTERS
- FABRIC MAKERS
- MOTOR CYCLISTS
- FINISHERS
- DRIVERS—Motor Transport
- WIRELESS OPERATORS

and Radio Direction Finding Operators

Daily Gleaner (*Kingston, Jamaica*), 15 August 1944

Courage and perseverance: these are mild enough words for the response of these settlers to the treatment they endured in Britain during those early years.

Let's leave aside the incidental hazards of the first few days. Some had their pockets picked or their luggage stolen, but that's something that might happen to any of us in a strange country. Let's concentrate on the basics.

The settlers needed two things above all. They needed a roof over their heads; and they needed to find work. How did they fare? Let me quote to you some of the poignant reminiscences brought together ten years ago in that eloquent booklet *Forty Winters On*, published by Lambeth Council.[1] Do you remember how that booklet got its name? In 1948 the Labour government's colonial secretary Arthur Creech Jones, had said airily of the *Windrush* settlers that they wouldn't survive their first winter in this country.[2] *Forty Winters On* told how they did survive.

May Cambridge

'People trudged for miles in search of a job and somewhere to live — only to be rejected again and again', said May Gertrude Cambridge, who told of signs saying 'NO IRISH, BLACKS OR DOGS'. These signs 'are no myth', she added. 'Sometimes you would knock on the door with a vacant sign in the window, some would say the room had just gone, others would just slam the door in your face while the less forthright wouldn't bother opening the door but you could see the curtains twitching.' James Lofters tells of a Caribbean settler who was knocking

James Lofters

17

on doors in search of a room to live in: 'At one home, the owner pointed to a nearby phone box and told him to use that.'
Some coped with this predicament by joking about it, like the character in A. G. Bennett's *Because They Know Not* (1959):

> Since I come 'ere I never met a single English person who 'ad any colour prejudice. Once, I walked the whole length of a street looking for a room, and everyone told me that he or she 'ad no prejudice against coloured people. It was the neighbour who was stupid. If we could only find the 'neighbour' we could solve the entire problem. But to find 'im is the trouble! Neighbours are the worst people to live beside in this country.

But if they laughed they were laughing to keep from crying.

What was it like once you did find a place to live? May Cambridge tells how six or seven people had to share the facilities. You'd have to queue in the kitchen with your pot to cook — but, after all, you were lucky to have a roof over your head. 'People had to share rooms and even the cellars were used.'
Claude Ramsey tells us: 'My first home in England was a house in Notting Hill Gate shared with about 30 other people, with only one bath and toilet between us. The conditions were appalling.' Tenants were subjected to rules and regulations 'fit for army recruits'. May Cambridge tells us that one of her landladies charged a penny for toilet tissue, and that if the lights were left on after a certain hour you'd get a knock at the door. You also had to be in at a certain time and all clothing had to be washed and

Claude Ramsey

dried in the bedroom. According to Walter Lothen, 'The landlords used to search the rooms when you used to go to work and stole rings and things like that.'

Some settlers found work before they left. Others had to find jobs on arrival.

Finding a job was an equally lengthy and frustrating task. Lynette Findlater said: 'The Labour Exchange sent you to vacancies but employers would say the job was filled or somebody was due to start. But the following day the Labour staff would inform you the vacancy was still open.'

When you did find a job, it was highly unlikely to correspond to your skills. Though only a small proportion of the settlers were unskilled — one in eight of the men and one in 20 of the women —

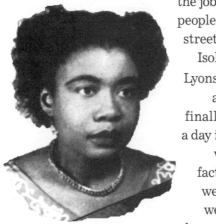

the jobs they secured were those that white people didn't want, such as sweeping the streets, general labouring, night-shift work. Isolyn Robinson got a job washing up at a Lyons Corner House for £4 2s. 6d. (£4 12½p.) a week. Lynette Findlater said: 'When I finally got a job I had to work 12 to 14 hours a day in horrendous conditions for less than white workers.' That was a job in a jam factory, working a 53-hour week for £13 a week. May Cambridge summed it up: 'We were given the most menial jobs and the lowest pay with no redress.... We were seen

Isolyn Robinson

as slave labour.'

In short, in both housing and employment the Caribbean settlers were pushed, remorselessly and deliberately, to the bottom of the heap. And not only in housing and employment. People need a roof over their head and they need work. But they also need to eat. So what happened in the shops? Very often shopkeepers would ignore a black customer and serve the white customer first although the black customer had been in the shop first. May Cambridge said : 'I once asked for a piece of salmon to be told it was too expensive for me to afford, and the shopkeeper made no effort to serve me.'

Lynette Findlater

Yes, you needed courage and perseverance in plenty to stand up to this kind of racist insult and discrimination day in and day out, year in and year out — especially when the insults and discrimination were stimulated by the activities of fascist gangs, which began with chalked slogans such as '*Niggers Keep Out*' and '*Keep Britain White*' and climaxed in the so-called race riots of 1958. Still more did you need courage and perseverance when the insults and discrimination were encouraged by the naked racism of the British police and by state racism, at first covert but at length codified in that legislation of the 1960s.

The Men from Jamaica Are Settling Down

'*YOU COULDN'T MEET A NICER CROWD*'

From PETER FRYER

THE large marquee near Clapham deep shelter was taken down yesterday. The people of Clapham will miss the colourful ties and cheerful smiles of their Jamaican guests.

The group of immigrants has been steadily dwindling as more and more left to take up jobs and go into private lodgings.

Of the 500 who came across in the Empire Windrush three weeks ago, 240 placed themselves in the hands of the Colonial Office. All but 30 of these have been found work.

These have gone to a hostel at Peckham, and they, too, will soon start work.

How are the Jamaicans settling down? That was the question I set out yesterday to answer, in conversation with the men themselves and with those who have come into contact with them.

First, the testimony of a Ministry of Labour official in charge of a large number of hostels in Onslow Square, South Kensington—a man who works amid a babel of tongues belonging to a dozen different nationalities.

"You couldn't wish to meet a nicer crowd," he told me. "They are cheerful and willing, and we have had no trouble of any kind, nor do we expect any."

A moment later he added reflectively: "Of course, I'm against all this colour bar. I've travelled about the world too much for that . . ."

Daily Worker,
14 July 1948

Refused Rooms

Some of the Jamaicans have, it is true, come up against colour prejudice—from a cafe proprietor here, a landlady there.

"Two fellows booked lodgings by phone." I was told. "When they went round to see the place they were told: 'Sorry we made a mistake.' The rooms were already let.'"

But these are the exceptions. Mr. Festus J. Fairweather, who began work on Monday as a welder, spoke with appreciation of the efforts of Ministry of Labour officials to place him and his friends.

"We've had a few difficulties," he said with a broad smile. "But we'll hold on until we settle. Of course, I have to wait a fortnight for the first pay day—the firm keeps a week's money in hand. But I'll make out."

Figures given to me by the Colonial Office show that 76 have gone to work in foundries, 15 on the railways, 15 as labourers, 15 as farm workers, and ten as electricians. The others have gone into a wide variety of jobs, including clerical work in the Post Office, coachbuilding and plumbing

21

NOTTINGHAM M.P.s URGE CURB ON ENTRY OF IMMIGRANTS

DIFFICULTIES FACING COLOURED PEOPLE

From Our Correspondent

NOTTINGHAM, AUG. 26

Two Nottingham M.P.s to-day criticized Britain's " open door " policy which allows unrestricted entry of people from other parts of the Commonwealth.

Mr. James Harrison, Labour M.P. for Nottingham North, referring to the fight in Nottingham on Saturday between white and coloured people, said : " This policy of allowing people to come freely into our country was practicable in the nineteenth century. It is completely impossible under modern conditions."

He felt that the keen competition for housing and " the ominous unemployment trends which now face immigrants " were problems which could be dealt with only at Government level.

VISIT TO INJURED

Before leaving for London to seek an interview with the Home Secretary to discuss Saturday's clash, Lieutenant-Colonel J. K. Cordeaux, Conservative member for Nottingham Central, visited a hospital to see some patients who were injured in the fighting. He called on other constituents who had also been involved.

" I have believed for some time that there ought to be something in the nature of a quota or definite restrictions on people coming into this country from oversea," he said. " I have been worried about this matter for some time because I feared that something serious like this might occur. What has happened emphasizes the seriousness of the position and the urgency of the matter. I want to put that before the Minister."

Later to-day Colonel Cordeaux had talks in London with Miss Hornsby-Smith, Parliamentary Under-Secretary, Home Office, to discuss last Saturday's incidents. The West Indian Government sent two industrial relations officers to the British Caribbean Welfare Service to conduct a two-day investigation. They met Captain A. Popkess, the Chief Constable, this morning and then went on a tour of the trouble spots, speaking to white and black residents.

WHY RACIAL CLASH OCCURRED

HOPE OF PREVENTING NEW OUTBREAK

FROM OUR SPECIAL CORRESPONDENT

NOTTINGHAM, AUG. 26

Will the ill-feeling engendered by the fights between coloured and white people here on Saturday night die down, or will it build up again later ?

The police acted promptly to quell what could have been an ugly racial conflict, and they are determined to see that it does not happen again, but already it is being murmured in the St. Ann's Well Road area —where the trouble occurred—that there are bound to be reprisals from the whites on the coloured population for the injuries inflicted. Is it, then, to become a vicious circle of " an eye for an eye," or can the city revert to its former good relations with its 3,000 coloured population ?

" I am surprised it has 'not happened before, but I am surprised that it happened here," Mr. A. F. Laird, chairman of the local consultative committee for the welfare of coloured people, told your Correspondent. That expresses the general view of Nottingham, a city that has a ratio of about 100 white to every coloured person.

Until now the city has lived amicably with the problem of people of different colour and temperament coming to live among them, for except for some initial opposition to the employment of coloured busmen, which was overcome, Nottingham has had no apparent colour bar.

ENVY AND FEAR

The reasons for friction have not varied greatly from those of other cities in Britain faced with the same problem—envy, resentment, and sometimes fear of eventual domination of white by black, but people have felt there was less difficulty here than elsewhere.

There have undoubtedly been niggling pinpricks on both sides; the white population in the St. Ann's Well Road area, which is only one of many in the city and its outskirts where the coloured people have congregated, complain that they are elbowed off the pavement by groups of young coloured men, and that girls are accosted and molested. The coloured people, for their part, maintain that they are humiliated and sometimes beaten up by white " toughs "; the police believe that such an incident last week brought on the reprisal on Saturday night.

Then there is the envy. Some of the coloured people earn good wages and buy small houses and cars, but their happy-go-lucky temperament shows in a way that irritates many white people, particularly those of low intelligence—in a " flashy " car instead of a " sober " one, radios at full volume into the early hours of the morning, and people whistling and calling to each other from their houses and lodgings. There is also sexual jealousy—the sight of

coloured men walking along with white women. The coloured men, too, tend to resent it when their actions, perfectly natural in their own country, are misunderstood over here.

None of these things in itself is likely to set race against race; but a sudden hit-and-run attack by a group of irresponsible West Indians armed with knives and other weapons on individual white men and women, and rumour and gossip spreading rapidly—these set a match to gunpowder.

About 430 coloured people are unemployed at the moment out of the total of some 2,000, and the number is rising; it is hard to visualize the despair these people feel, for contrary to some opinion the great majority of them came here to get work and not to " sponge " on the welfare state. But that does not seem to have a great bearing on the recent disturbance.

It seems that Nottingham, of all the towns with a colour problem, was just unlucky on Saturday. Every responsible person with whom your Correspondent discussed the situation expressed the hope that common sense, allied to determined police action, would prevent another outbreak. But " reprisals " from either side could easily spark off a bitterness and tension between white and coloured that could not be so quickly controlled next time.

At the moment, citizens of both races in parts of Nottingham await the next few weeks with unease.

CHAPLAIN TO WEST INDIANS IN BRITAIN

' TERRIBLE LOT OF WORK ' TO BE DONE

FROM OUR SPECIAL CORRESPONDENT

With one of the most cheerful smiles you could hope to see in a grey terminus, and carrying a large umbrella and a typewriter, the Rev. Ronald Campbell stepped off the Ocean Liner Express at Waterloo station yesterday morning into one of the toughest jobs in Britain.

Mr. Campbell has come from Jamaica to be chaplain to Britain's West Indian population.

The typewriter and the umbrella struck your Correspondent as handy symbols for

The Rev. Ronald Campbell.

Mr. Campbell's work as he outlined it. First of all he has got to settle in—to a country with grey skies in August which is very different from his own. " I want to meet as many West Indians as possible first of all," he said. Then the typewriter will come into play; he is conscious of a " terrible lot of work."

Mr. Campbell, who is a tall, slim man, 43 years old, was a printer before he took holy orders in 1950. In London he will be attached to the parish of his former archdeacon in Cornwall, Jamaica, the Rev. George Fox, at St. Etheldreda's, Fulham, which is a centre for many of his countrymen. In the first place he will work in the London area—the dioceses of London and Southwark. But later he hopes to travel to all parts of Britain where there are substantial West Indian communities.

Mr. Campbell will stay in London for a year, and may stay longer. For the moment he has left his wife and four children in Jamaica, but they may come to England later.

His appointment springs from the recommendations of a committee set up by the Archbishop of Canterbury, which found that many West Indians who had been regular churchgoers at home found difficulty in establishing contacts in Britain. Mr. Campbell will not only be available to help his countrymen find such contacts, however. He regards it as an equally important part of his work to help English people who have groups of West Indians in their parishes to understand them and cater for their needs.

The Times, 26 August 1958

RACE CLASH IN NOTTINGHAM " ALARMING "

OFFICIAL VISIT TO TROUBLE DISTRICT

FROM OUR CORRESPONDENT

NOTTINGHAM, AUG. 25

Two industrial relations officers of the Caribbean Welfare Services in London arrived in Nottingham to-night to investigate for the Caribbean Governments the inter-racial disturbances which broke out in the city on Saturday.

They are Mr. David Muirhead and Mr. Horford Scott. They will stay for two days and meet the Chief Constable of Nottingham, Captain A. Popkess, in addition to going into the trouble area and talking with West Indians.

Mr. Muirhead said: " We are here to try and see that no further similar incidents will happen in the future. There has never been a clash of such proportions in this country before. It was most alarming."

An emergency meeting in Nottingham to-night by leading West Indians appealed to the city's white and coloured residents not to take the law into their own hands. With tempers running high after the disturbance in which eight white people were taken to hospital the West Indians fear that more fighting may break out.

WEST INDIAN'S APPEAL

Mr. Eric Irons, a West Indian who has been in Britain for 14 years and who sits on the Nottingham Council of Social Service Consultative Committee for the Welfare of Coloured People, said after the meeting : " We have been to see the Chief Constable because we are so shocked at the incident which occurred over the weekend—I would call it a provoked incident.

" During the time we have been in this city (since 1949) we have experienced complete harmony between the races in spite of any personal misunderstandings. We therefore appeal to all sections of the community, both coloured and white, to use every restraint and to report to the police any provocation which may again be the cause of disturbances and bloodshed."

Commenting on his reference to provocation, he said : " I think the original incident was when a West Indian was going home from a party. A crowd of white men in a car actually stopped him and gave him a good beating up. It will be better to get harmony than to try anything like that which might provoke further clashes."

YOUTHS' RAID ON CAFÉ " LIKE EARTHQUAKE "

FIVE ORDERED TO PAY £200 COMPENSATION

Five young men found Guilty at London Sessions of causing malicious damage to a café at Shepherds Bush, W., owned by a coloured man, were each ordered to pay £40 compensation. The café-owner, Mr. Samuel A. Thomas, said in evidence that a five-minute raid by between 20 and 30 youths " was just like an earthquake." He added: " I didn't try to stop them because I would have been killed if I had."

The five men were Walter William Cook, aged 23, electrician, of Braybrook Street, Shepherds Bush; Leslie George Edwards, aged 21, porter, of Emlyn Gardens, Shepherds Bush; Roy Ernest Lyne, aged 21, labourer, of Sullivan Court, Fulham, S.W.; Peter Thomas Saunders, aged 17, apprentice plater, of Wilsham Street, Notting Hill; and Michael Philip Walsh, aged 18, salesman, of Cromwell Grove, Hammersmith. They were conditionally discharged for 12 months. Besides £40 compensation each was ordered to pay 10gns. towards the costs of the prosecution.

A sixth youth, Derek Frederick Handcock, aged 18, electrician's mate, of Talbot Grove, Hammersmith, was found Not Guilty and discharged.

Announcing the penalties, Mr. H. J. Hamblen said: " Had there been any personal violence towards Mr. and Mrs. Thomas you would most certainly have gone to prison."

The Times, 27 August 1958

POLICE REPORT ON OUTBREAK

COLOURED PEOPLE'S "REPRISAL"

FROM OUR SPECIAL CORRESPONDENT

NOTTINGHAM, AUG. 25

The fighting which flared up here on Saturday night was a reprisal by coloured people for previous incidents recently when some of their number were attacked by white men, the local police said to-day. Mr. F. D. Porter, assistant Chief Constable of Nottingham, told a Press conference that a number of coloured people had been interviewed but no charges had yet been preferred.

Police patrols, some with dogs, had been strengthened in the area—the St. Ann's Well Road district—and there will be stand-by squads until the authorities are satisfied there will be no more outbreaks. There were no reports of any trouble last night. "We are determined to stamp it out," Mr. Porter added.

Over 80 policemen were drafted into the area on Saturday night when it was estimated there were more than 1,000 people milling about, A preliminary report has been submitted to the Home Office by Captain A. Popkess, the Chief Constable.

Answering a protest made by the Fire Brigades Union Mr. Porter said that the fire brigade was informed by a radio officer when he saw the size of the crowd and the seriousness of the situation. At the time there were two or three police officers to about 1,500 people.

One fire engine turned out, but hoses were not used. "It was an ugly, riotous crowd and fires could have been started," Mr. Porter commented. "Had the hoses been used they would have been used by the police and not by the firemen."

Mr. Charles Coyne, aged 25, factory worker, who was stabbed four times in the back while on his way home, and is in hospital at Nottingham, was said yesterday to be much better.

PROTEST OVER USE OF FIREMEN

A protest is being made to Mr. R. A. Butler, the Home Secretary, by the Fire Brigades Union, after firemen with hoses were called to the inter-racial fight at Nottingham on Saturday night. Mr. Butler has been told that the union take "the gravest view" of the incident.

Mr. John Horner, the union's general secretary, said yesterday that the deputation will ask the Home Secretary "to give clear instructions to the nation's police and fire services not to use firemen as riot squads.

"It is not the function of members of fire brigades to quell public disorder. If the police require the use of fire fighting equipment, they should apply to local authorities for it, and use it themselves."

The Times,
26 August
1958

UNIONS WANT BALLROOM BAN: CHAIRMAN DENIES COLOUR BAR

From Our Special Correspondent

Mr. C. L. Heimann, chairman of Mecca Ltd.—dance halls, restaurants, public houses, and catering contracts (84 lines of them in the London telephone directory alone)—gave your Correspondent his reflections yesterday on the vexed subject of "colour bars" and the treatment of coloured customers on his premises.

He was commenting on the resolve of Sheffield Trades and Labour Council, which represents 100,000 workers, to ask Sheffield City Council to withdraw the licence of his Locarno ballroom there and the Musicians' Union to "blacklist" it on account of alleged "racial discrimination." Supporting the moves which were suggested by the Amalgamated Engineering Union, the secretary of the trades council, Mr. Vernon Thornes, reported that the management of the hall had referred him to the company's head office in London.

PARTNER RULE

If these threats in the north caused Mr. Heimann concern at the Southwark headquarters of his empire he gave no hint of it. He called the request to withdraw his licence "fantastic," and seemed rather hurt that anyone could confuse the policy he had personally instructed his managers to adopt at Sheffield, Nottingham, and Birmingham a couple of months ago with anything remotely resembling a "colour bar."

He did not know of any colour bar in any of his 30 dance halls. There were simply certain restrictions—"a coloured boy has to bring his own partner, black or white." He is not allowed to "pick up" another girl afterwards. No such limitation is placed on "white" boys.

If not exactly a "bar" all that sounded remarkably like at least a "colour restriction," did it not ? Mr. Heimann thought it would be true to say that, but he posed the problems which could arise otherwise in a hall with 600 white boys, 600 white girls, and 100 coloured boys without partners.

He insisted he had no objection to coloured people as such. He would take the same step, if need be, with Irish, Scots, or Jews. It was really a question of mixing with strangers. "Man from the beginning of time has always been suspicious of a stranger."

He emphasized, too, that this was "only a temporary measure" made absolutely necessary by "nasty fights" and the like. Also that the rule was working "perfectly": plenty of coloured boys were still coming in (with "lady friends") though, of course, fewer than before. It had not been necessary, so far, to introduce anything of the sort into his restaurants or public houses, and in many dance halls (the Royal at Tottenham, for instance) they had never had any trouble.

Why not ? Mr. Heimann could only think of one explanation. "Some towns," he said, "are more hot-headed than others."

BIRMINGHAM APPROACH BY TRADES COUNCIL

Birmingham Trades Council are negotiating with Mecca, Ltd., over restrictions on the admission of coloured people to their ballroom in Birmingham. Coloured men are admitted only if they bring their own partners, and according to the management many coloured couples accept these terms without complaint.

At the last meeting of the trades council, a resolution was submitted from the King's Heath branch of the Amalgamated Engineering Union calling on the council to organize a public campaign "to oppose this policy of dividing workers by the use of the colour bar." The motion was withdrawn after Mr. G. Varnom, the president, said there was more chance of securing removal of the restrictions by friendly negotiation than by formal protests.

THE CARNIVAL QUEEN'S ATTENDANTS

A coloured boy and a coloured girl will be two of the attendants for Miss Susan Martin, Malvern's Carnival Queen, when she heads the carnival procession through the town's streets on Saturday. The carnival is being organized by students from the Ministry of Supply College of Electronics in the town.

"MADE TOUR ATTACKING COLOURED MEN"

NINE YOUTHS REMANDED ON WOUNDING CHARGE

Nine young men, charged at West London Court yesterday with unlawfully and maliciously wounding a coloured man with intent to cause grievous bodily harm, were remanded in custody until Saturday.

Detective Sergeant M. Walters said that he had seen all nine and told each that he was believed to be one of about nine or 10 young men who between 3 a.m. and 5 a.m. on Sunday toured the Notting Hill district and "assaulted several coloured men with iron bars and similar weapons." He said all nine were charged with wounding Joseph Welch at Shepherd's Bush Green.

Sergeant Walters said that there was an objection to bail owing to the serious nature of the charge and the evidence in support of it, and the serious injuries sustained by three men still in hospital. The men before the court would be further charged with similar offences.

"Some of the victims of these assaults are seriously hurt and are in hospital, and one has what is believed to be a stab wound in the back."

Subsequently each of the accused made statements under caution which the prosecution suggested were a complete admission of this and other similar offences, the sergeant said.

The Times,
28 August
1958

REPORT

OF THE

WEST INDIA ROYAL COMMISSION,

WITH

SUBSIDIARY REPORT

BY

D. MORRIS, Esq., D.Sc., C.M.G.

(ASSISTANT DIRECTOR OF THE ROYAL GARDENS, KEW)

(APPENDIX A.),

AND

STATISTICAL TABLES AND DIAGRAMS, AND A MAP.

(APPENDIX B.).

𝕻𝖗𝖊𝖘𝖊𝖓𝖙𝖊𝖉 𝖙𝖔 𝕻𝖆𝖗𝖑𝖎𝖆𝖒𝖊𝖓𝖙 𝖇𝖞 𝕮𝖔𝖒𝖒𝖆𝖓𝖉 𝖔𝖋 𝕳𝖊𝖗 𝕸𝖆𝖏𝖊𝖘𝖙𝖞.

LONDON:
PRINTED FOR HER MAJESTY'S STATIONERY OFFICE,
BY EYRE AND SPOTTISWOODE,
PRINTERS TO THE QUEEN'S MOST EXCELLENT MAJESTY.

And to be purchased, either directly or through any Bookseller, from
EYRE AND SPOTTISWOODE, EAST HARDING STREET, FLEET STREET, E.C., and
32, ABINGDON STREET, WESTMINSTER, S.W.; or
JOHN MENZIES & Co., 12, HANOVER STREET, EDINBURGH, and
90, WEST NILE STREET, GLASGOW; or
HODGES, FIGGIS, & Co., LIMITED, 104, GRAFTON STREET, DUBLIN.

1897.

[C.—8655.] *Price 2s. 8d.*

*   *   *

The subject of tonight's meeting is 'The Politics of *Windrush*'. I make
no apology for having devoted my first few minutes to the human
side of the story. For this human side too is politics. Politics, as I see
it, is only marginally about political parties and MPs and ministers,
and presidents who can't keep their hands off women or off vodka
bottles. Politics is essentially about power. It's about who has the
whip hand over whom. And the *Windrush* pioneers were in a
certain sense powerless. That's why they were made to suffer. That's
why they were insulted and reviled and victimised and
discriminated against.

What they did have, what enabled them to endure that suffering
and come through triumphant, was what I have called courage and
perseverance. Or, to put it another way, the only kind of power they
had was staying power.

But if we are to understand the political essence of the entire
Windrush experience, we must first of all answer the question: 'Why
did they come here?' They certainly didn't come, as Diane Abbott
remarked of her parents in her first House of Commons speech,
because they wanted to 'swamp' anybody's culture. Nor did they
come because they saw the 'Mother Country' as a land flowing with
milk and honey, or London as a city paved with gold. With all due
respect to Clare Short, the people of the Caribbean have never lusted
for 'golden elephants'.

To put it in a nutshell, the settlers came to get away from chronic
hunger and poverty that had become unendurable.

Here we need to remember a little history.

For several hundred years certain Caribbean islands and
mainland territories (Belize and Guyana) were part of the British
Empire, and most of them were used mainly for the production of
sugar. Until the 1830s that sugar was produced by slave labour
transported from Africa. After emancipation most of the freed
slaves refused to work on the plantations any longer, so from then
until 1917 the planters used indentured labour from India.

PART III.

CONCLUDING OBSERVATIONS AND SUMMARY.

i.—OBLIGATIONS OF THE MOTHER COUNTRY.

510. In Parts I. and II. of our Report we have expressed the opinion that the sugar industry in the West Indies is in danger of practical extinction; that no industry or series of industries can in the space of a few years supply its place; and that some of the Colonies will for a time be unable to meet the necessary and unavoidable cost of administration, including payments on account of the public debt. We have also recommended the adoption of measures having for their object the substitution of other industries for the cultivation of the sugar-cane, and the general amelioration of the economic condition of the people, as well as the relief of the distress which may arise in many places.

511. The carrying out of our recommendations must involve the expenditure yearly of a considerable sum of money which the Colonies will, in their altered condition, be unable to provide. The more depressed the condition of any Colony may be the greater will be its need for additional funds and the less will be its ability to raise them from its own resources, and we consider that in one form or another pecuniary sacrifices by the mother country on behalf of the West Indian Colonies are inevitable.

512. Justification for this view can no doubt be found in the nature of the relations which exist between a mother country and such dependencies as Your Majesty's West Indian possessions. But in this instance we desire to draw attention to peculiar circumstances, which, in our opinion, impose a special and an unusually strong obligation upon the Home Government.

Exceptional circumstances of West Indian populations

513. The black population of these Colonies was originally placed in them by force as slaves; the race was kept up and increased under artificial conditions maintained by the authority of the British Government. What the people were at the time of emancipation, and their very presence in the Colonies at all, were owing to British action, or to the action of other European nations for the results of whose policy the United Kingdom assumed responsibility on taking possession of the territories in question; we could not, by the single act of freeing them, divest ourselves of responsibility for their future, which must necessarily be the outcome of the past and of the present. For generations the great mass of the population must remain dependent upon British influence for good government, and generally for the maintenance of the progress that they have made hitherto. We cannot abandon them, and if economic conditions become such that private enterprise and the profits of trade and cultivation cease to attract white men to the Colonies, or to keep them there, this may render it more difficult for the British Government to discharge its obligations, but will not in any way diminish the force of them. We have placed the labouring population where it is, and created for it the conditions, moral and material, under which it exists, and we cannot divest ourselves of responsibility for its future.

Loss to West Indies caused by exceptional conditions profitable to Great Britain.

514. There is also another consideration, which in our opinion ought not to be overlooked. The distress, which is beginning to be felt by the population; the difficulty in which some of them are already, or may soon be placed, of finding a livelihood; the still more certain difficulty of providing for their government and education, will be due to the failure of the sugar industry, which is in turn partly due to the protective policy of other countries and to the bounties which some of them grant on the production or export of sugar. To some extent at any rate these bounties and this policy have made sugar cheaper outside the countries in question, a result by which the British consumer has gained very largely. Whilst, therefore, it is unfair to say that the cause of the depression in the West Indies is due to any act of the British Government, we cannot overlook the fact that the British people have been reaping great benefit from precisely that set of circumstances which has been a factor in bringing the West Indies to the verge of serious disaster.

Conclusions reached by the 1897 West India Royal Commission

Indentured labour was a polite term for what was in fact serf labour. Indenture was simply slavery under another name, as the author of the standard work on the subject, Hugh Tinker, recognised when he called his book *A New System of Slavery* (1974).

British imperialism saw its Caribbean colonies as 'the tropical farms of the English nation' and said so: these were the words of a Royal Commission in 1884.[3] And those 'tropical farms' practised single-crop agriculture: a truly crazy system under which much of the food that should have been grown locally had to be imported from the 'Mother Country' at wildly inflated prices. Nearly 50 per cent of the food eaten in Trinidad came from overseas.[4]

Under imperialism there was no industrialisation. For instance, ground-nuts and coconuts were, or could have been, abundant in the islands, but there was no local industry devoted to extracting their oil and making soap from it.

Under imperialism there was no development. There was no progress. There was stagnation. The British West Indies were a neglected backwater. There was gross economic imbalance.

- In Jamaica, the British firm of Tate and Lyle owned 60,000 acres and produced one-third of the island's sugar; yet 92 per cent of the island's farmers had holdings of between one and 28 acres, while 170,000 day labourers either had plots of less than an acre or owned no land whatever.
- In Trinidad, two giant firms, Caroni (a subsidiary of Tate and Lyle) and Sainte-Madeleine owned 24,000 acres, while 80 per cent of the farmers had holdings of less than 10 acres and 30,000 farm workers had no land at all.
- In Barbados, St Vincent, and elsewhere, the pattern of inequality was exactly the same.[5]

Those small proprietors and landless farm workers, the beasts of burden in those 'tropical farms', were people of African and Indian descent; and another Royal Commission, in 1897, admitted that the labouring population of the British West Indies were living in what they called by the genteel word 'distress'.[6]

Apart from sugar, the crops produced on those 'tropical farms' were grinding poverty, disease, illiteracy, slum housing, and a staggering rate of infant mortality. Here is how Eric Williams, in his book *From Columbus to Castro: the History of the Caribbean* (1970), summed up social conditions in the British West Indies in the 1930s:

> The Barbadian labourer was fed worse than a gaolbird; he could not afford milk in his tea; said the planters, he did not like milk!... The daily consumption of fresh milk in Kingston, Jamaica, with its 30,000 children of school age, was one-fifteenth of a quart per head; the Jamaican politicians in the age of colonialism said the Negroes preferred condensed milk.... An official picture of Trinidad in 1937 described every adult over twenty years of age as affected by deficiency diseases, and the working life of the population reduced by at least one-half.... What, then, of the children? With the mother debilitated by hook-worm, half-starved and vulnerable to waterborne diseases, the infant mortality rate was staggering. For Trinidad it was 120 per 1,000 live births; for Jamaica 137; for Antigua 171; for St Kitts 187; for Barbados 217; as compared with 58 in England.... Of the total deaths in Jamaica in 1935, over 33 per cent were of infants under five years of age. An examination of 12,000 schoolchildren in Kingston revealed that 40 per cent were undernourished.[7]

WATERFRONT STRIKES IN JAMAICA

FROM OUR CORRESPONDENT

KINGSTON (JA.), MAY 10

Strikes of waterfront workers broke out at Kingston yesterday, and another occurred on the north side of the port. The latter was settled without any increase of pay, but at Kingston stevedore labour obtained better conditions. A Dutch shipping company had brought labourers in a ship from Curaçoa to unload the cargo, but the strikers prevented their doing so.

The strike riots in Westmoreland Parish were discussed at a meeting of the Kingston Corporation.

Councillors declared that they did not want a commission from England; the men here were capable of handling the situation. It was desirable that the Government should be comprehensive in their effort to improve conditions due to unemployment and low wages.

MARCH BY UNEMPLOYED

FROM OUR CORRESPONDENT

KINGSTON, JA., MAY 12

The labourers at the city wharf struck to-day for an eight-hour day and increased pay, and it is feared that a general waterfront strike may develop.

A larger body of unemployed marched this morning to the site of the proposed township contemplated in the Government's housing plan in the hope of being employed in road-building. Finding that operations had not begun, they then marched to the Colonial Secretariat and sent a deputation to the head of the competent department to express their disappointment.

When work was begun some hours later there were more applicants than jobs. The unemployed, though dissatisfied, say that they are not prepared to make trouble.

THE JAMAICA RIOTS

FROM OUR CORRESPONDENT

KINGSTON (JA.), MAY 13

At the coroner's inquest yesterday on the bodies of those who were killed when the police fired on an attacking mob of strikers at the Frome sugar estate, the jury found that no one was criminally responsible for the deaths.

It is uncertain whether the Captain-General, Sir Edward Denham, will be able to embark for England on leave on May 24, owing to the unsettled conditions. The authorities are satisfied that there is no trace of Communist influence in the Colony; the discontent is purely economic.

The Times, *11 May 1938*   The Times, *13 May 1938*   The Times, *14 May 1938*

In the 1930s the lid blew off. People had had enough. There was an upsurge of social unrest and strikes and demonstrations. This upsurge gripped

- *Belize* (then called British Honduras) in 1934-35, and spread to
- *Trinidad* in 1934 and 1937,
- *Guyana* (then called British Guiana) in 1934 and 1939,
- *St Vincent* and *St Lucia* in 1934,
- *St Kitts* in 1935,
- *Barbados* in 1937, and
- *Jamaica* in 1938.

The Times,
31 May 1938

LABOUR UNREST IN BRIT. GUIANA

NO DISTURBANCES

In a message to the Colonial Office Wilfrid Jackson, Governor of British Guiana, states that there is no truth in the report [not in *The Times*] of riots and disturbances in that Colony on Friday. There were partial stoppages of work or in the last fortnight, which in one case developed into almost complete stoppage but with very few exceptions all concerned returned to work after a day, and the police were not called in. Generally the situation is that there have been some local stoppages during the last few weeks settled without disturbance by the assistance of the Labour Department. stoppage of the Labour Department and in most cases some a ques-e, while in other cases some adjust-t any change.

TWO KILLED IN RIOT

KINGSTON, JAMAICA, June 3.—Two persons were killed and three injured when police fired on a looting mob at Islington, in St. Mary's Parish, this morning. Six persons were arrested. Sherwood Foresters were sent to the scene and made seven further arrests.—*Reuter.*

CONTINUED ANXIETY IN JAMAICA

TROOPS FIRE ON MOB

Mr. C. C. Woolley, the Officer Administering the Government of Jamaica, telegraphing on Thursday to the Secretary of State for the Colonies, reports that, while the satisfactory situation in Kingston has been maintained, conditions continue to give cause for anxiety in the parishes, where much unrest, accompanied by some lawlessness, is reported, and the police, fully supported by the military, are being taxed to the utmost.

Sherwood Foresters patrolling Saint Elizabeth and Clarendon, the report says, were obliged to open fire on a mob obstructing communications, and two of the mob were wounded. No casualties are reported elsewhere.

The Times,
4 June 1938

JAMAICA DISORDERS

WARNING TO LAWLESS ELEMENTS

FROM OUR CORRESPONDENT

KINGSTON (JA.), JUNE 5

Mr. C. C. Woolley, the Officer Administering the Government, has issued a warning against the continuance of the disorders which are the work of a criminal element. The Government, he says, are determined to use the sternest possible measures for the suppression of lawlessness. No improvement of any of the conditions affecting the lives of the people can be expected unless law and order are restored. He invites the people to rely on negotiations, and not on force, and also to accept the services of the Conciliation Board. The latter is considering the problems of the country parishes as earnestly as it did the case of Kingston.

Mr. Woolley announces that as the real development of Jamaica and the permanent solution of unemployment must be through intensive agriculture, the Government intend to spend £500,000 on land settlement. A Department is to be set up to devote attention to this question. The need of unemployed to become settlers has received special consideration.

FIGHT WITH LOOTERS

The police were compelled to use firearms in the Islington District of St. Mary on Friday. Rioters were looting shops when a carload of police arrived. The latter were pelted with stones and other missiles, rifles and bayonets of the police were smashed, and constables were injured. One rioter aimed a shotgun at the sub-officer in charge of the squad. The rioter was shot dead before he pulled the trigger. Three other members of the mob were killed and one wounded. The arrival of troops enabled the police to arrest 13 persons.

Several planters are leaving St. Mary, taking their families with them, owing to the threatening attitude of the strikers, and also owing to looters, who belong to the criminal class.

An attempt was made to burn the Catholic church at Annotto Bay, where the demonstration was widespread. Elsewhere there were two attacks on the police with firearms. At the western end of the island the demonstrators say they do not wish to give the police trouble; their only object is increased pay. Eleven of the 14 parishes have been affected by labour troubles in the past four weeks.

Centres have been established from which heavily armed mobile patrols can be sent to any part of a parish at the shortest notice. There are rumours that additional strikes will be called to-morrow. H.M.S. Ajax has gone to Montego Bay.

The Times, 6 June 1938

In Jamaica the struggle developed into an open rebellion that lasted for three months. Jamaican workers and farmers downed tools, marched in demonstrations, looted shops, cut telephone wires, put up road-blocks, tore down bridges, burnt crops, besieged the rich in their houses and, armed with nothing but sticks and stones, fought back against armed police and troops.

- Britain's colonial governors screamed for warships, marines and warplanes;
- 46 people were killed (including 14 in Barbados, 12 in Trinidad, 12 in Jamaica, and 3 in St Kitts);
- 429 were wounded; and
- thousands were thrown in jail.

CRUISER REACHES JAMAICA

STRIKERS SING NATIONAL ANTHEM

FROM OUR CORRESPONDENT

KINGSTON (JA.), MAY 26

H.M. cruiser Ajax arrived here to-day, to find that the island, apart from the continuance of the waterfront strike itself, had very nearly reverted to normal.

Mr. Norman Manley, the barrister who offered his services as a mediator in the waterfront strike, continued negotiations to-day with 2,000 men who assembled on Government Pier. He seemed to be making some progress, and when the meeting adjourned he granted the strikers' desire that he should lead them, as loyal British subjects, in the singing of the National Anthem.

At the moment the position is that some shipping representatives are prepared to pay another 2d. an hour to the dockers, making 11d. for those who work in ships' holds, and 10d. for those who work on the wharf. The strikers, however, demand a uniform 1s. an hour, and the latest agitation is that the strike should continue until the labour leaders in custody are released. Meanwhile, steamers continue to leave Kingston unloaded, although incoming vessels are able to discharge at Cristobal.

DIFFICULTIES OF NEGOTIATION

Mr. MacDonald, Secretary of State for the Colonies, in a written reply to a Parliamentary question, yesterday, reported further information he had received from the Governor of Jamaica. This gave the casualties over a period of three days as two killed and 78 injured (one seriously). Of the injured, two are members of the public assaulted by the mob, four are police constables, and two are special constables. The police generally, the report states, had exercised great restraint.

The Governor (Mr. MacDonald added) is prepared to set up a conciliation board, of which the Commissioners now inquiring into labour conditions and rates of wages would be members. It has not hitherto been possible to get leaders of labour to make definite proposals to Government, or to form a responsible trade union with which the Government could negotiate, but the Governor has now received an undertaking that the representations of the labourers regarding wages will be put forward.

MORE JAMAICAN STRIKES

TROOPS SENT INTO THE INTERIOR

FROM OUR CORRESPONDENT

KINGSTON (JA.), MAY 30

Troops have been sent into the interior of the island as it is feared that trouble will spread in the district west of Mandeville. In Kingston all is quiet, but armed patrols are still on duty.

A general waterfront strike is threatened at Savlamar. At Frome, where a short and peaceful strike had been settled by granting the strikers' demands, it is likely that all the labourers will cease work again to-day.

The Conciliation Board has decided to match the wage increases granted to the Kingston longshoremen with increases for banana-handlers at all the ports.

The Times, *31 May 1938*

The Times, *27 May 1938*

30

It is surprising, to say the least, that throughout the 1980s, half a century after these events, there was little recollection of them — and none here in Britain that I was aware of. Yet they had some important consequences.

One immediate consequence was the appointment of yet another Royal Commission, chaired by Lord Moyne, a scion of the Guinness family who was later to be appointed colonial secretary.

In 1938-39 the Moyne Commission travelled all round the Caribbean, investigating social conditions in Barbados, British Guiana, British Honduras, Jamaica, the Leeward and Windward Islands, and Trinidad and Tobago. The Commission submitted its

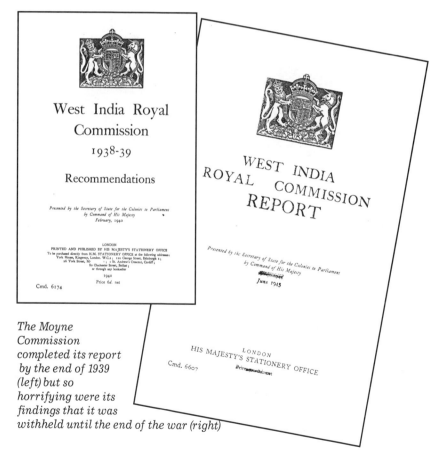

The Moyne Commission completed its report by the end of 1939 (left) but so horrifying were its findings that it was withheld until the end of the war (right)

Crowds assembled in the grounds of Queen's Park, Bridgetown, Barbados, to listen to the proceedings of the Moyne Commission relayed by loudspeaker. (Moyne Report, 1938-39)

report at the end of 1939, but it was such a revealing, indeed devastating, document that the British government thought it better to leave it unpublished until the end of the war.

It was at last published in June 1945, and the picture it painted of the British West Indies and its citizens' lives was indeed horrifying. In some parts of the British West Indies, it said, rates for agricultural labourers were little better than the shilling-a-day introduced after emancipation one hundred years before. In the towns, things were hardly better: 'The condition of many of the

At the outbreak of war most of our Report was already in draft, and we were faced with the choice either of completing it on the basis of the evidence in our possession and of the decisions reached at our discussions during the summer of 1939, or of attempting to take into full consideration the influence of war conditions on the West Indies. It has not of course been possible, particularly in the Chapters dealing with the export trade of the West Indies, to overlook the immediate consequences of a state of war, and although we decided to adopt the former alternative we have nevertheless been obliged to make certain consequential changes in the appropriate sections of our Report. Our decision to report as soon as possible on the basis of the evidence before us was taken partly because the adoption of the second alternative would have involved the reopening of many questions and a considerable and needless prolongation of our enquiry; but in a much greater degree because we believe that the early publication of our Report and, as we hope, action, by Your Majesty's Government in the spirit of our recommendations, will be a valuable earnest of the good intentions of the citizens of the United Kingdom towards the colonial peoples in their charge. We were also influenced by the view that the fundamental problems of the West Indies will remain, and cannot be permanently affected by abnormal war conditions. It is to the solution of these fundamental problems that we have directed our enquiry.

A passage in the 1938–39 Moyne Report discussing its delay

townspeople, as we saw for ourselves, is pitiable.' About education the Moyne Commission had this to say:

An examination of the working of the educational system … reveals serious inadequacies in almost every respect. There is not nearly enough accommodation for the children who attend schools; and these include by no means all the children of school age. Existing accommodation is frequently … in a chronic state of disrepair and insanitation. Teachers are inadequate in number, and are in most Colonies not well paid. Their training is largely defective or non-existent.

Domestic Science room, St Philip's Girls' School, Barbados (Moyne Report, 1938-39)

A one-room school building, Windward Islands (Moyne Report, 1938-39)

Schoolroom, St Kitts (Moyne Report, 1938-39)

Handicrafts and Housecraft block, Mason's Hall, Tobago (Moyne Report, 1938-39)

Housing in Bridgetown, Barbados (Moyne Report, 1938-39)

Chronic sickness among the people of the British West Indies was common, mainly because of 'deplorable' housing:

> It is no exaggeration to say that in the poorest parts of most towns and in many of the country districts a majority of the houses is largely made of rusty corrugated iron and unsound boarding; quite often the original floor has disappeared and only the earth remains ... sanitation in any form and water supply are unknown in such premises, and in many cases no light can enter when the door is closed. These decrepit houses, more often than not, are seriously overcrowded, and it is not surprising that some of them are dirty and verminous in spite of the praiseworthy efforts of the inhabitants to keep them clean. In short, every condition that tends to produce disease is here to be found in a serious form. The generally insanitary environment gives rise to malaria, worm infection and bowel diseases; leaking roofs, rotten flooring, and lack of light encourage the spread of tuberculosis, respiratory diseases, worm infections, jigger-lesions and rat-borne diseases; overcrowding, which is

Anguilla, Leeward Islands (Moyne Report, 1938-39)

Housing on a sugar estate, Trinidad (Moyne Report, 1938-39)

usually accompanied by imperfect ventilation, is an important agent in contributing to the high incidence of yaws, tuberculosis, venereal diseases and, to a certain extent, leprosy.[8]

New workers' housing in concrete on a sugar estate in St Lucia, Windward Islands (Moyne Report, 1938-39)

New workers' housing in timber; Bauxite works, Mackenzie, British Guiana (Moyne Report, 1938-39)

Rural housing, Trinidad (Moyne Report, 1938-39)

Rural housing, Nevis, Leeward Islands (Moyne Report, 1938-39)

During the war these horrifying conditions had got worse, not better. Throughout the British West Indies the cost of living had almost doubled. There was widespread unemployment, but those without jobs got no dole whatever.

In Jamaica, the hurricane of 1944 had destroyed most of the banana, coconut, and coffee crops. People were hungry. People were desperate. Young men and women could see no future for themselves. They looked for a new and better life in the 'Mother Country', whose citizens they were and to whose passports they were entitled.

And there you have the answer to the question: 'Why did they come here?' 'They' came *here* because 'we' were *there*.

Or rather, that is half of the answer. It tells us what pushed them. But there was also a pull, in the shape of recruitment campaigns —

Daily Gleaner *(Kingston, Jamaica),*
22 August 1944

The Times, *27 October 1944*

newspaper advertisements — urging Caribbean people to come and work in Britain.

- London Transport ran one such campaign.

- The British Hotels and Restaurants Association ran another.

- A Minister of Health by the name of Enoch Powell welcomed Caribbean nurses to Britain.

London Transport Museum

Mr Charlie Gomm selecting and interviewing the first batch of applicants for London Transport, Barbados 1956

"I came in from cricket on a Saturday night, and on the radio London Transport wanted these people urgently, and I got up on a Monday morning and went and registered... I was in Hackney Garage the following week."

Keith Hunte was recruited as a bus driver in 1961

From "Sun a-shine, Rain a-fall". London Transport's West Indian Workforce. *(London Transport Museum, 1994)*

London Transport was the first organisation to set up a scheme to recruit staff directly from the Caribbean. In 1956 LT opened a recruiting office in Barbados, and the Barbadian government lent new recruits the fare to Britain which was then paid back over two years through LT. Trinidad and Jamaica followed with direct recruitment in 1966. Other major employers, including British Rail and the National Health Service, introduced similar programmes. Although the 1962 Commonwealth Immigration Act restricted the number of people coming to Britain, LT's direct recruitment continued until 1970.

Daily Gleaner
(Kingston, Jamaica),
6 October 1955

And yet at the same time, in secret Cabinet discussions, there was talk of a 'coloured invasion', of an 'influx' of black people. Look at the figures.

- Between 1948 and 1953 the number of Caribbean migrants entering the UK never exceeded 2,300 in any one year.
- In the years 1955-60 the annual figure varied between 16,000 and 26,000.
- Only in 1960 and 1961 did the figure rise above 50,000. And there was a reason for that increase: by that time it had become clear that immigration controls would be introduced pretty soon, so settlers' families came over to join them before it was too late.
- And even then, in 1962, the year of the first racist Commonwealth Immigrants Act, the Caribbean and African population in Britain totalled just 135,000.

Some 'invasion'! Some 'influx'!

To visit the Public Record Office and read the reports of those secret Cabinet discussions on immigration control is to enter a world of the most vile and paranoid racism on the part of both government ministers and those who advised them. Early in 1955, as Harold Macmillan later revealed, it was Churchill himself who suggested 'Keep Britain White' as a good slogan for the Conservatives in the forthcoming general election.[9]

In the years 1953-56 there were three separate working parties

RENEWED CALL FOR CHANGES IN IMMIGRATION LAW

CONSERVATIVE M.Ps' FEARS: "SEEDS OF ANOTHER LITTLE ROCK"

From Our Political Correspondent

The Times, 28 August 1958

Seeing in the Nottingham fight between coloured and white people on Saturday night a red light warning of further troubles to come, some Conservative M.P.s intend to renew their demand for control to be placed on immigration from the Commonwealth and colonies when Parliament reassembles in October.

After the questions and debates raised on this subject last session the Government arranged that officials in the departments concerned should consider all aspects of this problem, and these consultations have been going on for some time. Thus, when the matter is raised again, Mr. Butler, the Home Secretary, will be in a better position to reply to M.P.s and to put the problem in perspective.

A resolution on the subject is on the agenda for the Conservative Party conference. It has been tabled by Mr. Norman Pannell, Conservative M.P. for the Kirkdale division of Liverpool, who obtained the signatures of about 30 Conservative and two or three Labour M.P.s for a motion (never debated) during the last session of Parliament. This expressed growing disquiet over "the continuing influx of indigent immigrants from the Commonwealth and colonies, thousands of whom have immediately sought National Assistance."

BASIS OF RECIPROCITY

It asked the Government "to amend the immigration laws on the basis of reciprocity with Commonwealth and colonial territories, all of which both impose restrictions on the entry of nationals of the United Kingdom and reserve the right to deport such nationals for grave misdemeanours."

Such a suggestion has several times been made in debates, but Government spokesmen have always deplored it; they believe it is essential for Commonwealth unity and future good relations with the colonies as they come forward to Commonwealth status that British subjects arriving in the mother country should not be subjected to controls.

Mr. Pannell said yesterday that he had engaged in correspondence with the Home Secretary, the Commonwealth Relations Office, and the Colonial Office, and they all rejected the idea of control. "They say that it is a controversial question which would require legislation and they are not prepared to introduce it at the moment," he said. "Yet all colonial and Commonwealth countries impose restrictions on immigrants from the United Kingdom and reserve the right to deport them for certain offences. In a Commonwealth of equal partners, we should have reciprocal legislation. The situation is deteriorating rapidly in Britain as a result of the unrestricted influx and the time has come to impose some restriction."

"EVIL RESULTS"

"The Nottingham fighting is a manifestation of the evil results of the present policy and I feel that unless some restriction is imposed we shall create the colour bar we all want to avoid. Unless we bar undesirable immigrants and put out of the country those who commit certain crimes we shall create prejudice against the immigrants, particularly the coloured immigrants. We must avoid this.

"The object of my representations is to get some control, not to bar all colonial and Commonwealth immigration, but to see that the immigrants shall not be a charge on public funds, and that they are deported when guilty of serious crimes."

Mr. Pannell has called attention to the fact that of the 130 convictions for living on immoral earnings in the Metropolitan police district in 1957, 66 were convictions of British citizens from the Commonwealth and the colonies (Malta, 35; West Indies, 15; West Africa, 13; and three others).

12 MONTHS' HALT

Another Conservative, Mr. Cyril Osborne, M.P. for Louth, has been pressing the Government to take powers to exclude immigrants who are unfit, criminals, or idlers. He admits that there are many Conservative M.P.s anxious to strengthen Britain's links with the Commonwealth and colonies, who oppose him, but he believes that action will eventually have to be taken through force of circumstances. He often makes the point that there are 500 million British subjects who are technically entitled to come in.

"In the next Queen's Speech I would like to see the promise of a complete prohibition on Commonwealth and colonial immigration for 12 months—making exception for bona fide students—until the matter is sorted out," Mr. Osborne said yesterday. "If we do not do it, and there is serious unemployment, the trade unions will impose the rule 'last in, first out' and there will be trouble. It will be black against white.

"We are sowing the seeds of another 'Little Rock' and it is tragic. To bring the problem into this country with our eyes open is doing the gravest disservice to our grandchildren, who will curse us for our lack of courage. I regard the Nottingham incident as a red light to us all."

USE OF FIRE BRIGADES

Commenting on criticisms made about the arrival of firemen with hoses on the scene of the fighting in Nottingham, a Home Office official said yesterday that in the Fire Service Act, 1947, there was no provision which specifically laid it down that a fire brigade cannot be used to assist the police in the event of a civil disturbance. No special guidance on this point has been sent out by the Home Office.

Mr. Butler, who is keeping the Prime Minister informed about the Nottingham fighting, yesterday was considering the further reports he has received from the local police. It is possible that he may send out some guidance to the police and the fire service about the use of fire-fighting equipment in quelling public disorders. He has not yet replied to the request of the Fire Brigades Union that he should receive a deputation from them. They have protested about the calling of the fire brigade, and have requested that instructions should be issued making it clear that fire brigades are not to be used as riot squads.

discussing the so-called 'influx', which they saw as 'an ominous problem'. They sought advice from the police and from managers of labour exchanges. This is what the Metropolitan Police told them in 1953:

43

> On the whole coloured people are work-shy and content to live on
> national assistance and immoral earnings. They are poor workmen....
> They are said to be of low mentality and will work only for short
> periods.

Managers of labour exchanges in the Midlands reported in the
same year that black workers were 'physically and temperamentally
unsuited to the kind of work available in industrial areas'. The
labour exchange managers had this to say about black women:

> It is reported that they are slow mentally and find considerable
> difficulty in adapting themselves to working conditions in this
> country. The speed of work in modern factories is said to be quite
> beyond their capacity. On the other hand they have been found to give
> fairly reliable service as domestics in hospitals, institutions and
> private domestic employment.[10]

The Cabinet, in those secret discussions, had a big dilemma: how
to stop black people with British passports from entering Britain
while allowing white Australians, Canadians, and so forth to come
here freely. They couldn't discriminate in this way openly. They had
to discriminate without saying they were doing so. At length they
came up with an ingenious solution to their dilemma. This solution
was a system of work permits. A prospective employer would have to
seek permission for the entry of a named immigrant. This would
exclude almost all black immigrants and would frustrate any
accusation of discrimination on the ground of skin colour.
Immigration officials would have complete discretion to refuse
entry to 'undesirables'. The new regulations would be rigorously
applied only at ports where Caribbean people normally arrived. And
this nasty arrangement could be presented as 'impartial'.

This was the racist blueprint put into effect by the 1962 Act. In
1962 state racism was enshrined in British law for the first time.
And that gave the green light to the police in their consistently
abominable treatment of black people.

CALL FOR AMNESTY

The Churches are seeking an amnesty for long-stay families facing deportation from Britain, if they fulfil certain conditions.

Owen Lashley lived in Britain from age 16 to 27, then returned from Barbados with his wife, Lorraine, in 1988. Elder daughter Magdalen is at university here now; younger daughter Takita (7) was born in Britain. Owen and Lorraine are qualified youth and community workers in Manchester and had started their own business. The whole family faces deportation.

The Churches are calling for an amnesty for potential deportees who fulfil the following:

A person who has lived in the United Kingdom for at least five years and EITHER is the parent of at least one child born here who has lived in the UK for a minimum of two years OR is self-sufficient in terms of income and housing.

The Churches Commission for Racial Justice is also urging an amnesty for those who claimed asylum in this country before the end of 1993 and whose claims have still not been determined.

Churches Commission for Racial Justice, Inter-Church House, 35-41 Lower Marsh, London SE1 7RL
Tel: 0171 620 4444   Fax: 0171 928 0010

After a campaign for amnesty, the Lashley family were told in 1998 that they had permission to stay in Britain

45

New Nation
6 July 1998.

The smug,
smiling arrival
of the five
Lawrence
suspects at the
public inquiry in
south London on
30 June 1998
contrasts with
their departure
(below): 'spitting,
snarling and
covered in coffee
and rotten eggs'.

Daily Mail, Wednesday, July 1, 1998

THE ANGRY FIVE SUSPECTS LEAVE THE INQUIRY INTO TEENAGER'S MURDER

Fighting back: Luke Knight (left), Neil Acourt (second left, partly obscured), David Norris (centre back), Jamie Acourt (throwing punch) and Gary Dobson (back right)

Daily Mail, *1 July 1998. Last year the* Mail *published pictures of the five suspects, naming them as Stephen Lawrence's killers*

The police are in fact the cutting edge of the racist state. Over the years this has been proved over and over again, in case after case, in report after report.

By one of history's sly ironies, the 50th anniversary last June of the coming of the *Windrush* coincided with the climax of the first stage of the inquiry into the murder of Stephen Lawrence. At the very same time as the BBC was belatedly doffing its cap to the *Windrush* pioneers, and just as the Post Office was belatedly issuing stamps featuring participants in the annual Notting Hill carnival, these tributes were eclipsed by the Lawrence inquiry's revelations about police incompetence, police inefficiency, and police racism.

Fifty years after *Windrush*, the last few days of the Lawrence inquiry's first stage were like the lancing of a boil. What came out stank to high heaven.

Neville and Doreen Lawrence leaving the Stephen Lawrence Inquiry with lawyer Imran Khan after Sir Paul Condon gives evidence. October 1998.

And those belated apologies, from the second-in-command of the Metropolitan Police and, later, from the Commissioner himself, Sir Paul Condon, did nothing at all to sweeten the stink of year upon year of corruption and cover-up.

Condon's apology is not enough, say Lawrences

FIVE YEARS after Stephen Lawrence was murdered, Sir Paul Condon, Commissioner of the Metropolitan Police, apologised in person yesterday to the teenager's parents for failing to catch the killers.

His comments were dismissed by Stephen's mother, Doreen, as patronising and she repeated her call for his resignation. There could be no way forward for Britain's largest police force while he was in charge, she said.

Giving evidence to the official inquiry into the death of Stephen, 18, Sir Paul admitted a number of his officers were racist. Yet he repeatedly dismissed suggestions that the force was "institutionally" racist and denied that racism was responsible for the botched investigation into Stephen's death near his home in Eltham, south-east London.

"I deeply regret that we have not brought Stephen's racist murderers to justice and I would like to personally apologise again today to Mr and Mrs Lawrence for our failure," Sir Paul said.

"We have heard people have been saying and I accept that a central concern is that the Met is racist. I acknowledge that we have not done enough to combat racist crime and harassment."

But he added: "If I believe that racism or corruption has impacted this case in any way, I would have already said so. I sincerely believe these issues did not influence this tragic case."

At times he was clearly embarrassed as he suffered persistent heckling from the Lawrence family supporters ("Condon, you're leaking") and tough questioning from the inquiry panel.

On other occasions his performance bordered on farce as he struggled with phrases such as "identify the mischief" and "the challenge facing us"

BY ANDREW BUNCOMBE

rather than refer directly to racism. Throughout the two hours and twenty minutes he spent at the inquiry it seemed that he was fighting to save his career.

Delivering his prepared speech, the Commissioner appeared reasonably at ease, outlining a series of reforms to counter racism within the police. He said the Deputy Assistant Commissioner, John Grieve, former head of the Anti-Terrorist Unit, had recently been appointed to head a new section dealing specifically with violent and racial crime.

But during the question-and-answer session he was less assured. He was repeatedly asked by the panel to admit the force was institutionally racial. Sir Paul refused to do so, denying that he was using "weasel

INSIDE
Why we think the police are racist, page 3
The canteen culture, page 3,
Race attack costs Los Angeles $24m, page 3,
Leading article, Review, page 3

words" but claiming that using such a label gave the wrong impression and would be harmful.

In one dramatic exchange, a panel member, Richard Stone, recalled South Africa's Truth and Reconciliation Commission and Bishop Desmond Tutu's offer to Winnie Mandela to confess her crimes. "Just say 'Yes, I accept institutional racism exists'," he was urged. "I think a lot of people here are willing you to say that."

After a noticeable pause, Sir Paul countered: "The answer is that it would be very easy to please the panel and the [other] people here to say such

a thing exists. I believe it would be dishonest for me to say that just to please you."

The panel also asked Sir Paul why he had informed the public as far back as 1993 that there had been no problems with the investigation when that was clearly not the case. The panel said Mr and Mrs Lawrence had found the attitude of officers investigating their son's murder, in April 1993, patronising.

Stephen's parents were clearly angered by the Commissioner's performance. Mrs Lawrence said: "Sir Paul has got fine words. I still have not been given the answer as to why Stephen's killers are still free. As I sat listening to Sir Paul this morning the word [introducing came up in my head. I think it is just a PR job.

"For five years we have still not been given justice ... I think he should resign and I think he should be asked to go."

She said she had met the mother of David Norris – one of the five men suspected of killing her son – last weekend at a south-east London branch of Marks & Spencer. "I cannot explain what I felt," Mrs Lawrence said.

"It has taken me the whole weekend and I still have not got over the shock of it."

Stephen's father, Neville Lawrence, added: "I have been waiting patiently to hear Sir Paul Condon come here today and admit the wrongs that have been done to our family.

"It is now five years and families are still facing the things that we faced."

Lee Jasper, secretary of the National Assembly Against Racism, said: "Anti-racists and black communities are deeply disappointed by the evidence presented by Sir Paul Condon. It is not possible for the Met to make a few tinkering, cosmetic changes and expect that everything is business as usual."

Sir Paul Condon, Commissioner of the Metropolitan Police, at the Lawrence inquiry yesterday   David Rose

Independent, *2 October 1998*

Condon's last-ditch denial that there was institutional racism in the Metropolitan Police contrasted strangely with the admission a little later by David Wilmot, chief constable of Greater Manchester, that institutional racism does exist in his force.[11]

My force is racist, police chief says

Manchester chief constable admits officers reflect society

David Pallister

THE Chief Constable of Greater Manchester, David Wilmot, yesterday accepted that institutional racism existed in his force — an admission that will reverberate throughout the British police service.

Giving evidence at the Stephen Lawrence inquiry in Manchester, Mr Wilmot said that "overt and internalised" racism had to be eradicated.

"We have a society that has got institutional racism. Greater Manchester Police, therefore, has institutional racism. Some of it is not of the overt type; it's that which has been internalised by individuals and it's our responsibility to try and make sure that it is eradicated."

His remarks — which are in contrast with previous evidence from the Metropolitan Police Commissioner, Sir Paul Condon — were welcomed by Stephen's father,

Neville Lawrence. He said: "It is good to see he's admitting to institutional racism and that they are willing to take steps to try and stop it. Now I want to hear how he's going to do it and how to promote black officers up the ranks where they can make a difference.

"I would like to know if Sir Paul is listening to some of the things happening up here and if he's prepared to look at his position."

A spokeswoman for the Met argued that the two police chiefs were using different definitions. "The commissioner was talking about institutional racism as being a matter of policy which means that all police officers go to work with a racist agenda."

Mr Wilmot did make it plain that he was not branding all his 7,000 officers as guilty. "I think that the vast majority of our staff are working hard to remove racism," he said. He told the inquiry that about 2.6 per cent of his officers were from ethnic minorities, compared with 6 per cent of the conurbation's population. The highest ranking officer was a chief inspector.

As the inquiry has progressed the definition of racism embedded within an institution has become a semantic minefield, as the chairman, Sir William Macpherson, pointed out yesterday.

"I don't like the term because you ask a dozen people about the definition and you get a dozen answers," he said. But he added: "There is a reluctance to accept that it is there, which means that it will never be cured."

Mr Wilmot, both at a lunchtime press conference and before the inquiry, which has moved to an hotel in central Manchester, accepted that the issue had to be confronted. "As long as you deny the problem you are not going to seek solutions," he said.

turn to page 2, column 8

Guardian, *14 October 1998*

To say the least, there is some inconsistency here. But where crimes against black people are concerned, the police are highly consistent, in five ways:

1. They are unwilling or reluctant to investigate;
2. They are slow in getting to the scene;
3. They are unwilling or reluctant to prosecute;
4. They give misleading advice; and
5. They treat the victims of crime as criminals themselves.

The fact of the matter is that, in the eyes of the police, from the highest ranks right down to the bobby on the beat, black people's lives are of less consequence than white people's lives and the murder of a black person is of less consequence than the murder of a white person.

How is this to be explained? Is it just a matter of casual racism? By no means.

In 1982 the then Metropolitan Police Commissioner, no less, let the cat out of the bag. He told an American journalist: 'In the Jamaicans, you have people who are constitutionally disorderly.... It's simply in their make-up. They are constitutionally disposed to be anti-authority.'[12]

49

This really gives the game away. The choice of words is highly revealing. Here, in the words of London's chief police officer, is state racism openly displaying its historical roots in Empire, in the imperialist system. To this high-ranking officer and his colleagues black people born in Britain are not British. They are 'Jamaicans', regardless of which island or territory their parents came from. That is to say, they are not fully-fledged British citizens but colonial subjects, who must be policed by the methods traditionally regarded as suitable for a British colony. Black people who come to the metropolitan country are relegated to colonial status. And so are their children and their children's children. It is as if the police were an occupying power in a hostile territory. That was, and still is, a basic premiss of police culture all over Britain.

Myrna Simpson, mother of Joy Gardner, outside the Old Bailey where three police officers were acquitted in 1995 of Joy's manslaughter

*   *   *

There came into my letter-box the other day a prospectus of lectures being given at Gresham College in the City of London. One course of four lectures, in November-December 1998, is entitled 'Dreams and a Special Destination: Fifty Years of Caribbean Migration to Britain'. The prospectus says: 'Compared to other migrations from the Caribbean the one to Britain has been marked by a perception of literary success and social, economic and political failure.'

It's not clear whether this is in fact the opinion of the organisers of this course. But it's certainly not my opinion. About 'literary success' there can of course be no doubt, bearing in mind the work of Wilson Harris, C.L.R. James, George Lamming, Caryl Phillips, and Samuel Selvon, to take five names more or less at random. And that list grows all the time. The *Times Literary Supplement* recently reviewed *Bernard and the Cloth Monkey* by Judith Bryan, which won the 1997 Saga Prize for an unpublished novel by a black British writer and has now been published by Flamingo. The *TLS* reviewer called it 'a brilliant and thought-provoking book.'[13] Judith Bryan is only one among many gifted young black British writers; and we shall undoubtedly be seeing many more.

But 'social, economic and political failure'? Failure?

No one can deny that black people still show up in disproportionate terms in all unfavourable social statistics; that they still find it harder to get work than white people; that they are still more likely than white people to suffer overcrowding; that black children are still less likely than white children to realise their full potential at school; that young black people are still more likely than young white people to be arrested; and that a disproportionate number of young black people are still sent to jail. But can we therefore speak of 'failure'? The very courage and persistence of which I spoke at the beginning point to anything but failure.

I'm not arguing that a handful of black MPs and black trade

One of the many protests against racist murders, portraying the mounting resistance to them

union leaders and black TV presenters are to be counted as magnificent successes. I don't think you can measure success in those terms. In the last analysis success isn't measured by role models or leaders.

But look around you. Look at the black community 50 years after *Windrush*; look at its capacity for getting things done. The Stephen Lawrence case is the outstanding example of what I mean. That inquiry, which — however painfully — brought into the light so much that authority had wanted to keep hidden in the dark, would not have happened without the quiet dignity and unflinching determination of Mr and Mrs Lawrence. Against all the odds they stood their ground, refusing to let their campaign be sidetracked or hijacked by either the White Left sects or the Black Muslim sect, insisting on their right to find out the full tragic circumstances of their son's death.

I don't call that failure. I call that success. And there are thousands and tens of thousands of Doreen and Neville Lawrences in the black community who are never again going to be victimised; who will never again be fobbed off by officialdom; who will never again bow the knee to authority; who are determined to stand up for their rights and to stand together in the common struggle against racism and against the system that spawns it.

Of course there are gigantic struggles ahead. Only this week we have had this shameful attempt on Channel 4 to brand black men as rapists. When you look at the 'evidence', it is based on a sample so small, over a time-scale so minute, that any social scientist, any statistician, any scientist worth his salt, would laugh it out of court. This isn't evidence. This is prejudice. This is racism going on and on and on.

But the *Windrush* settlers and their descendants have the human resources to face the coming struggles. And in those struggles they will have white friends and allies who no longer see themselves as the God-given generals and black people as merely the foot-soldiers, the hewers of wood and drawers of water, but are prepared to take their place in the ranks. C.L.R. James, one of the 20th century's greatest writers, who ended his days in Brixton, put it like this 60 years ago in his masterpiece *The Black Jacobins*: 'The blacks will know as friends only those whites who are fighting in the ranks beside them. And whites will be there.'

Val Wilmer

C.L.R. James

The *Windrush* generation and their descendants have wisdom and experience. They have courage and determination. Above all, they have the intelligence to turn personal pain and sorrow into solidarity and effective collective action.

That, in my view, is the chief political lesson to be learnt from this past half-century of British black history. And it is a lesson that all of us, whatever skin colour we happen to have been born with, need to learn and take to heart.

Inset: Clara Buckley at the Brixton meeting. Her son Orville Blackwood was killed in Broadmoor prison hospital in October 1981 after an injection. Clara has campaigned against the 'accidental death' verdict, because Orville 'was held down by bully boys and died within seconds'. She is seen with Arthur Scargill (left) at a 1993 miners' rally commemorating two pickets who died in the 1984-85 miners' strike

Protest against the killing of Joy Gardner when police tried to remove her forcibly from her home for deportation

Chair: There is an African saying that when a sage, an old person, is speaking, the young ones should take notice. We are deeply indebted to Peter Fryer for his in-depth study. Only yesterday the Channel 4 television programme about rape and young blacks came out [*Dispatches: Gang Rape*, Thursday 19 November 1998] but already Mr Fryer has made up his mind about this insidious racism, creating fear, especially among white people. We are a society of black, white, Asian people, working together. We have to begin to see inside the nature of things we see on television, we have to have an objective view.

Samuel Oduwole of Yaa Asantewaa Arts and Community Centre:

I'm glad to be part of the evening. I am dedicating this song, 'The Wind Rush the Ship' to the people who have been here before. First a poem:

Windrush

What is Windrush?

Windrush is the celebration of the 50th anniversary of the first migration to Britain on the SS *Empire Windrush*.

We, the third generation, are inspired by their courage, endurance and pride, of what they have experienced and been through.

Those experiences are like a woman who is pregnant and in labour and at the end of her pregnancy delivers a beautiful child as a result of her endurance.

We are the generation of that beautiful child, who are glad that their suffering during cold winters and sadness of leaving families and friends behind did not stop them from staying in Britain to make it better for us.

We the new generation congratulate them for the contribution that they have made in defending this country during the second world war.

We also praise them for their contribution in rebuilding the National Health, transport services and other industries after the war.

It is in reaching us, the third generation, through the story of their lives, that we fit into this legacy.

As we journey to a new life with understanding of the pathway, both culturally and spiritually, that led to those who came here before us.

We, the new generation, are grateful to them for all the good things that happened because they came to Britain.

© Samuel Oduwole

SONG: 'The Wind Rush the Ship'

1. The wind rush their ship.
As they journey from home
To the dream land they thought pave of gold (twice)

It's a life to celebrate
All that they have been through
When they look back
To those years again. (twice)

2. The wind rush their ship
For those who came before us
And for those things they went through in their
    time.
The wind rush their ship
For the pain they endured
And the ache they have felt in their time.

It's a life to celebrate, etc. (twice)

Samuel Oduwole

Interlude: The wind rush the ship
As they journey from home,
To the dream land they thought pave of gold. (twice)

3. The wind rush their ship
As their lives inspired us
They long for lives they have left behind at home
The wind rush their ship
As they fought for their right
They stood up high with their pride and dignity.

It's a life to celebrate etc. (Repeat the lyrics till it fades out)

© *Written by Samuel Oduwole for Windrush event in July 1998 (for performance)*

Question: When you were a reporter on the *Daily Worker*, you must have covered lots of stories. What was it that made you stay with it over the years and led to you writing a book [*Staying Power*]?

Peter Fryer: It made a big impression on me, at 21. It was the first time I had my byline on a story. I have a lot less ego now than I had then, but the first byline's always important, so that stuck with me. And you see, in the 1980s when the troubles came here in Brixton and in Bristol and elsewhere, when the children of people I had welcomed to Britain in 1948 were in trouble with the police and there were riots or uprisings, my own family, my own children who were about that age, said to me, during several discussions around the dinner table: 'Look, you have a moral responsibility. Suppose you had emigrated in 1948 and your children — us — were in trouble with the police. Wouldn't you think somebody ought to stick up for us? Why don't you write a pamphlet? You know something about black history.' I realised it was a moral imperative. I did have a responsibility.

Then I realised that if I was going to do the job, I couldn't mess with it and just do a pamphlet. I spent two-and-a-half years doing what turned into quite a big book, to discharge that moral responsibility. I felt I couldn't do otherwise. I had to do it, and of course from that other things developed. Mr Walker was very kind to call me an authority. I feel I'm just a John the Baptist for some future black historians from the black community itself, who will take the torch that I've lit and will carry it forward and write much bigger and more worthy books in the future.

Questioner One: I am appalled that [on the leaflet about this meeting] 'black' is spelt with a common 'b'. People should think a bit more carefully. It's saying we are second-class citizens.

Question: What is the likelihood of us in Britain having a 'Windrush Day', a day of celebration, where we down tools?

Chair: I said Brixton makes history. The green space opposite is going to be named Windrush Square. Perhaps the powers that be may decide to have a Windrush Day.

Questioner One: I don't think *Windrush* is something to celebrate. It should be marked and acknowledged.

Young woman in the audience: What about the people who came over here? Yes, my grandmother did do very low, menial work, but I've gone to university. Both my sisters are in college. My brother was in college. Now I think that was something to celebrate. We are not in a diseased condition in the West Indies. We are no longer picking and producing sugar for Tate and Lyle. We have to mark every hour, otherwise all of that was in vain.

Questioner One: It is to be marked. There is a big difference between celebrating and marking. My forefathers paved the way so that I could go to university. We need to be careful.

Chair: Some of these [matters] are very subjective. I know there is a discussion in the black community. I use lower case 'b' for black because if I'm going to use upper case 'B' for black I must use upper case 'W' for white.

Questioner (young woman, to Mr Denniston): When you came over during the time of the *Windrush* did you find that you became closer to Irish people because the situation they were going through was similar?

Mr Denniston: Jamaicans, especially building workers, come home and say they're better off with Irishmen because the Irishmen were more considerate and humane to them than Englishmen are. But I can remember that the first race trouble started with Irish men in Kilburn. They beat the life out of them.

Put all the jokes aside. It's quite nice to find a group of people who you think might be against you and they show you a little humanitarian treatment. But when it comes to me, if I can't beat the individual I just leave him. I don't expect anybody to fight my battle. Let them legislate, but if it's a fight, not me.

Question: I'm a journalist from Pakistan and I would like to ask Mr Peter Fryer: We support the historic struggle of Caribbean people facing the situation here. But what do you think about the present situation? Do you think that Caribbean people and other immigrants who came to this society fully take their responsibilities, as a responsible citizen of this society, when they are living here in the past ten to 20 years — Caribbean and other immigrants?

Peter Fryer: I prefer to use the word settlers. I have a stop in my mind about 'immigrants' because it's usually a pejorative term. I think 'settlers' is more neutral. [Do I think they] fulfil their responsibilities? Well, yes, I do. [LAUGHTER]

Question: After the catalogue of the horrifying things we have heard that you discovered in your research, do any of you have grounds for optimism?

Mr Denniston: Well so far, I know two millionaires. I'm hoping we have half a dozen by the end of the year. [LAUGHTER]

Peter Fryer: My answer would be that of the great Italian anti-fascist Gramsci, who said that it's necessary to have pessimism of the intellect and optimism of the will.

Chair: From my point of view, yes, I think there is [ground for] optimism. The reason I say so is from where I work. I work in the

Younger members of the audience with Mr Denniston and Mr Wilmot

Black Cultural Archives and every week I see young people come to the archives, both black and white, researching history. Most times they say to me: 'I did not know about this before,' or 'This is stereotyping.' You see both black and white students coming together, especially young women, they're more serious. They do their research and go out and write. You see them walking along in Brixton and I think there's a lot of grounds for optimism. I think especially the white young people and the young black people, there's a lot of intermixing with them. They have a more open outlook. My answer is: there are grounds for optimism.

Leroy Gittens: I do agree. I met this South African guy and we were talking. He said to me: 'We must learn to live like the hippopotamus and the crocodile.' It took me ages to [work] out, so I called him again. I said: 'What do you mean?' He said: 'To share the same waterhole, you got to live together. We share the same earth, we got to live together, because if we can't, we'll destroy each other.'

Samuel Oduwole: I want to talk as the art education officer in

Westminster, dealing with young people. Nobody knew about the *Windrush* until [the anniversary events] happened this year. The young people were really inspired. There were a lot of questions about what *Windrush* meant. I feel the government should mark *Windrush* [every year]. It will educate the young generation to know what has happened in the past, to have inspiration. So I wrote about it. I think it's important for the government to have in the calendar, to mark as an important event in the history of Britain.

Woman at back: I have a poem by a boy of eight, Craig Thompson.

WINDRUSH

I'm sailing the seas
I'm sailing the seas

I miss my family
And coconut trees
My bags are packed
I'm ready to go
I'm looking at the sea
It flows so slow

Good bye family
I'll be back soon
Follow the star
Also the moon

I'm frightened inside
and nervous too
I'm leaving my heart
In Jamaica with you

By Craig Thompson
Age 8

July 1998

© *Craig Thompson*

61

Mr Denniston: How old did you say he was? Eight? We ought to send him a Christmas present!

Nadia Cattouse: It's very difficult for me because while listening to Peter Fryer so many thoughts are in my head. I can speak, for instance, on the fact that as a young woman I came during the war and joined the British Women's Army and then I went back home, [to British Honduras, now Belize] and came back on the *Georgic*, this time to England. I'd been living in Scotland before, where I'd had really a ball; I had a wonderful time in Scotland. When I came to England it was to view these cards in the windows that Peter spoke about, and knowing that I was dealing with a different people, in a way.

Then by some strange chance I found myself working with a unit that was a liaison body between the people arriving and all those social statutory bodies. So I would go with various people and meet the boats, and meet the trains, and also we had an office where people wanted to find their relatives or find a job. I know a great deal about the endurance and determination, especially of the women, who would arrive and they would need a place for just that night to lay their heads. The next day they would walk the streets and they would talk to any black face they saw about getting a bed. But more than that, they would just go into a shop, sometimes in the Midlands they would go in a bus and say to the driver: 'Where are you going? Is there a factory at the end of that place?' 'Yes.' [They would] get on to the bus, go into the shop, into the factory, and say: 'I can do this and that, is there a job for me?' It used to really appal me in the last 20, 30 years when I would hear the young mouthing this idea that the older generation didn't do anything. Have you heard that? [YES!]

Many of this young generation did not understand that the tools and techniques that these older generation brought from the Caribbean, that's what they were using here. They had endured and struggled over there, they knew something about how to organise and how to carry themselves and they used those kind of techniques here. Later on came [ideas] from the United States and, watching television, came the marches and demonstrations. That was another way of doing something. But these young people who were saying that, I couldn't just see them for one minute being able to do what their grandparents had done. They, as individuals, could just go and be determined.

Ms Nadia Cattouse

One more thing I'll say: Had all the people coming from the Caribbean been willing to work as maids and gardeners, there would have been no problem. There were always loads of people phoning me up at this unit I worked for, asking: 'Oh, can I have a maid?' They thought this was plenty coming to them from the West Indies and each time I tried to explain: 'These are people who have got families back there. They've come here to make extra money because they've got to send it back to those families.' People got very angry with me on the phone. 'Are you Irish?' they would say to me. [LAUGHTER] One or two of them were very famous. They would spend holidays in Jamaica and saw the crowds of people as a wonderful opportunity for them to load their houses with maids and nannies and all the rest of it. But that's another thing.

One last thing I'd say: when Peter spoke of all these secret deliberations in the Cabinet, it wasn't so secret really, because you could hear and read every day in the papers speeches that were being made in parliament by various people. They were outrageous speeches and you would see clumps of people sitting around a table discussing *me*. They didn't know anything about me, they'd knock heads together and be talking in this intellectual way. This went on for years. Those speeches were made by people who were adored in the parliament. Enoch Powell was the man of the year, and this little Colonel Cyril Osborne from the north of England would repeat

Inset: Nadia Cattouse left home as an ATS volunteer in 1943. Below: Nadia with colleagues at the Signals School, Scottish Command, Edinburgh 1944

those speeches. It was quite clear to me that the police, the friendly bobby, began to see himself as the front line, as Peter said. And to this day, from then till now, that has not changed. They see themselves operating a policy that people in the government make.

Mr Allan Wilmot: I served in the Royal Navy and the Royal Air Force — Air-Sea Rescue Service. I left Jamaica in 1941 in the Royal Navy serving on minesweepers and convoy escort vessels. I transferred to the RAF in 1944. I came to England, did further training, and served in the British Isles. I can remember coming to Brixton, London, in 1947. You know, when I talk, people think I'm about 200 years old, as when I came to Brixton and looked around there were no other black faces in sight. Today, if you walk around the same place and see a white face — it's a tourist! [LAUGHTER]

I went home after the war ended and returned to England before the arrival of *Windrush*. I arrived at Southampton on 21st December 1947 on the troop transport ship *Almanzora*, but we weren't expected. When the *Empire Windrush* came the British government and the news media were alerted.

In my case we just came off the ship, and that was it. Today I think: 'Christ, how the heck did we survive?' Nowhere to live, nothing at all. As it was the Christmas period, everything was closed down. Anyway, we all struggled because most of us were ex-servicemen who were in this country

Mr Allan Wilmott. Below: with The Southlanders during his show-business days

before, so we were in a sense not really new. But being in the services, and now a civilian, is a different cup of tea, because being a serviceman you had a uniform, and a Service Club, and hostel accommodation available. But as a civilian — nothing at all. London Underground trains were our saviour, because that's where you used to sleep: on the train at the end of the line. The workers there saw our plight and turned a blind eye when we explained that we were ex-servicemen and homeless. Sometimes we used to go to Lyons Corner House, which was open 24 hours, and sleep over a cup of coffee. That was our routine until the Christmas holiday was over and things got a bit on the move. Then the *Windrush* came and that was our salvation. With the publicity and the large amount of people needing help, things had to

Marquees were erected on Clapham Common to assist the Windrush *arrivals*

be done immediately re work and accommodation, resulting in the reopening of the Clapham air-raid shelter.

I was one of the first black postmen in London in 1948. It's a long story. From then I turned political. I looked around and tried everything. I couldn't get a foothold because the general consensus was: once you're black a broom is available. Everywhere you enquire, there is a vacancy with a broom waiting, and if you're allergic to a broom, starvation sets in, 'cause finance is almost exhausted. So I had to bury my pride, and take a job washing plates at the Cumberland Hotel, Marble Arch, and then life got a bit better as our potential was suddenly realised by many.

I surveyed the scene and realised there were no black British in show business: it was all American black imports. I used to sing in school, and church choirs, school plays and RAF shows, so I says: 'Let me try my luck at that.' I got a breakthrough and that lasted for 27 years and then I decided to retire because I said to myself: 'Well, you're getting old, son, no big saving, or pension fund, and nothing on the horizon.' So I got a job at British Telecom as an operator and I did 17 years and retired with a pension.

Just when I retired it was around the same time the West Indian ex-servicemen and women, all advanced in age and not organised, realised the only way out is for collective recognition, so they decided to get together and form the West Indian Ex-Servicemen and Women's Association. I joined, became an executive officer, and today I'm the current president of the association.

But I can say that looking back, you had to have faith in yourself for survival. Quite a few packed up and returned home. They couldn't take the existing conditions. You are born in a country, and although you leave that country, you always dream of returning. Just like the Irish always singing about Ireland, but most never return. Well, the same thing applies to most West Indians. Deep down in your mind it's: 'I'm going back home someday.' For 95 per cent of the West Indians who came here, in their minds it was: 'Five years and go home.' Well most of us have done over 50 years. Five stretch out to 50-odd years, because after a while we start families. You think to yourself you don't want to go home and leave your families behind, so today we find ourselves survivors. Fortunately, those of us who made up our minds to stay put tried to give our children an education, because without those certificates you're nothing. That's why it grieves me when I look around and see the black youngsters walking around the streets window-shopping. You have to go for it. You got to study, pass your exams and don't go round and say: 'Because I'm black, etc.' OK, we will admit that racism is there, and does exist, but you've got to find a way to combat it, with a bit of success, and most important is to equip yourself educationally. If you go for a job you can't go there looking pretty, with no papers. You've got to have your CV and certificates. But if you hang around clubs and enjoy yourself instead of studying, you will find yourself on the scrapheap and wondering where you have gone wrong when it's too late, most of the time.

It hurts me when I walk around and see the young black children not studying, getting a little dead-end job, for pocket money. They rely on their parents and when that help dries up they find themselves doing petty crime and end up in a remand home which is full of black youngsters. They get documented and it leads

Left to right: Allan Wilmott, Nadia Cattouse, Oswald Denniston, Peter Fryer, Clara Buckley, Bill Boakes and Cyril Smith

on. If you go for a job, right away being previously in trouble, it goes against you. So my prayer is that the young black of this country wake up, because we, the pioneers, are more or less retired and the young ones should realise what is happening and do something positive. You will find the Asian kids take a different view of life in this society. Recently I have been to a prize-giving and the Asian kids were up front with prizes for achievement. They know that education is the key and if you want to get a good job you have to be in possession of some levels to be considered in most cases. So my hope for the future is that young blacks take an interest in education themselves. Thank you. [YES!]

Chair: Let's give a big hand to Arthur Torrington [Public Relations Official of the *Windrush* Foundation]. It's through his efforts that we saw all the things about *Windrush* on television. He was the person behind it, he was the organiser of all the events in London, Bristol, Manchester, of the reception with Prince Charles and many other public events. It was through his efforts and ingenuity that the whole thing about *Windrush* [took place]. We want to acknowledge your efforts, Arthur, and give you God speed.

Finally, please sign the visitors' book. I want to thank all of you, but especially Alison who has been videoing assiduously. Before we go we want to take several photos: Mr Fryer, Mr Denniston, Mother Cattouse and then the young ones ...

Four groups were involved in organising the meetings in Leeds and Brixton:

The **Black Cultural Archives** was set up in 1981 to collect, document, disseminate and preserve all historical records of the presence and socio-economic contributions of black people in Britain. Send us your archive material: family histories, ephemera, minutes of meetings, posters, flyers, etc. If you want to come to the archives, phone to make an appointment. Our exhibition area is open Monday–Saturday 10.30am–6pm (free)
Black Cultural Archives, 378 Coldharbour Lane, London SW9 8LF.
Tel: 0171-738 4591. Fax: 0171-738 7168.

Index Bookcentre specialises in black fiction and non-fiction, politics and children's books. We also stock paperback fiction, gender and media studies, college and school books. Redevelopment plans mean Index Bookcentre faces demolition. We oppose these plans and are campaigning to stay in central Brixton. Call in to browse, or to order your books on our fast ordering service.
Index Bookcentre, 10-12 Atlantic Road, London SW9 8HY.
Tel: 0171-274 8342.

Leeds Independent Labour Network is a movement seeking to unite those inside and outside the Labour Party to fight for democratic principles and a political perspective that shifts taxation from the poor to the rich. It is linked to like-minded organisations which have followed the lead of MEPs Ken Coates and Hugh Kerr, who have raised similar issues.
Leeds Independent Labour Network, c/o M. Christie, 22 Montague Crescent, Leeds LS8. Tel: 0113-293 1948.

The Movement for Socialism (MFS) aims to develop as a transitional organisation towards the creation of a new party for socialism. Its ideas are non-sectarian and internationalist. It aims to support, encourage, and assist wherever possible the struggles of the working class and all those in the world oppressed and exploited by the increasingly globalised power of capital; and to work for a truly human society in which the rule of capital is ended.
The Movement for Socialism, 4 Harvel Crescent, London SE2 0PW.
Tel: 0181-310 6005.

The politics of *Windrush*

AN emotional and historic meeting in Leeds brought Peter Fryer face to face with members of the Leeds African Caribbean Community who had come to Britain before and with Windrush, preparing the grounds for today's rich multi-cultural society.

Fifty years ago, the ship *Empire Windrush* brought the first major wave of settlers from the Caribbean. Peter Fryer, a correspondent of the *Daily Worker*, met them and wrote the only newspaper report of the event.

At Leeds' Mandela Centre, 100 people gathered to hear Fryer lecture on The Politics of Windrush.

Called by the Leeds Independent Labour Network, the meeting on 10 September was ably chaired by Councillor Norma Hutchinson.

The pre- and *Windrush* members of the audience spoke of their perseverance and hope in the difficult first years.

This multi-cultural inheritance was reflected in the very mixed nature of the audience, attracting over 30 African Caribbeans and several Asians.

Their strength and 'staying power' were the theme of Peter's powerful and emotional lecture.

They triumphed against ignorance and racism — a racism which came from the whole colonial history of Britain.

These black settlers knew more about British history than the history of their own lands. They were discriminated against in homes, jobs and even in shops and pubs.

Fryer explained the background to the exodus to Britain from the Caribbean.

There had been very little improvement in the lives of workers and small-holders since the abolition of slavery.

Wages had not improved over 50 years, infant mortality was three times the rate of Britain along with a considerably lower life expectancy.

Housing conditions were as bad any Victorian slum. Fryer quoted appalling statistics from British Government Royal Commissions.

From the mid-1930s the Caribbean people had had enough. A sugar monopolised economy which led to importing expensive food and household goods was destroying the basis of life on these highly fertile islands.

Colony after colony rebelled. Strikes and demonstrations were ruthlessly put down by the colonial governments.

Dozens died and hundreds more were imprisoned.

By 1938 another Royal Commission was formed. It came to the same conclusion as all the others -- that the Caribbean was wracked by endemic poverty, but the report was suppressed till after the second world war.

It was to escape these conditions that African Caribbeans came to Britain to seek a new life.

Their indomitable spirit and struggles led to their establishment in Britain.

They overcame not simply ignorance, but the institutionalised racism of the immigration laws.

This dignity and struggle is today epitomised in the struggle of the Lawrence family to obtain justice.

Lively discussion and questions followed the lecture.

Replying to one young black person who asked where he stood on the question of reparations, Fryer explained that as a socialist he was in favour.

However the damage of 400 years of the triangular trade and slavery could not be repaid even in part without dismantling the whole capitalist system.

This drew a loud round of applause.

Movement for Socialism Bulletin, September 1998

Peter Fryer with three veterans of the Windrush *era at the Mandela Centre, Leeds, 10 September 1998.*

Left to right: Glen English *was an RAF engine fitter from 1944 to 1948, and was one of the first black people to get an MBE. He founded the Caribbean Cricket Club.*

Noel Edwards *was an RAF motor mechanic from 1944 to 1948 and came to Britain on the* Windrush *He set up the Earl Grey Society to help settlers find accommodation in Leeds.*

Norma Hutchinson *chaired the meeting.*

Marcus Mitchell *was in the RAF Transport Unit from 1944 to 1948 and trained Territorial Army drivers in England for 12 years.*

71

Notes

1   A welcome new edition of *Forty Winters On*, with additional material, has been published as *The Windrush Legacy: Memories of Britain's post-war Caribbean Immigrants*, edited by Sam Walker and Alvin Elcock (Black Cultural Archives, 1998).

2   Arthur Creech Jones (1891-1964) was colonial secretary, 1946-50, and for many years chaired the Fabian Colonial Bureau.

3   *Report of the Royal Commission appointed ... to inquire into the public revenues, expenditure, debts, and liabilities of the islands of Jamaica, Grenada*, etc., pt IV, Supplementary Remarks (C. 3840-III, 1884), p. 16.

4   Daniel Guérin, *The West Indies and their Future*, trans. by Austryn Wainhouse (Dennis Dobson, 1961), p. 49.

5   Guérin, pp. 40-1. The figures for Jamaica date from 1943, those for Trinidad from 1946.

6   *Report of the West India Royal Commission* (C. 8655, 1897), p. 64.

7   Eric Williams, *From Columbus to Castro: the History of the Caribbean 1492-1969* (André Deutsch, 1970), pp. 450, 451, 454.

8   *Report of the West India Royal Commission*, 1938-1939 (Cmd 6607, 1944-45), pp. 32, 34, 92, 139, 174.

9   Harold Macmillan, *At the End of the Day 1961-1963* (Macmillan, 1973), pp. 73-4.

10 This and the two previous quotations are from documents in the Public Record Office. Full references are given in Peter Fryer, *Black People in the British Empire: An Introduction* (Pluto Press, 1988), p. 159 nn. 6, 8.

11 *Guardian*, 14 October 1998.

12 As quoted, *Policing London*, no. 2 (September 1982).

13 *Times Literary Supplement*, 11 September 1998.